THE BIRTH
that
COUNTS

**The Position of Our Redeemed Status Through
the Substitutionary Work of Christ**

DR. VELMA D. WHITE

ISBN 978-1-0980-3918-9 (paperback)
ISBN 978-1-0980-3919-6 (digital)

Christian Faith Publishing, Inc.
832 Park Avenue
Meadville, PA 16335
www.christianfaithpublishing.com

Printed in the United States of America

DEDICATIONS

To Jean Stewart, cofounder of Camp Living Water. You and Larry Stewart sacrificed so much for this camp to share the love of Jesus to generations of our Native children and youth.

To all the Camp Living Water ministry team. Your years of dedication and hard work of planting seeds year after year will be honored by the Lord of the Harvest.

To Osborn Ministries International. Thank you for exemplifying the power, yet simplicity, of True Gospel ministry to a hurting world.

To Reverend's Ross and Cyndy Assoon, Ashley Black, and Pastor's Len and Susan Paluwski. A new breed arising! Your love, dedication, and passion to serve Jesus is contagious.

ENDORSEMENTS

The Birth that Counts is a critical book for the entire body of Christ. Dr. Velma White kindly and candidly gives us a comprehensive look at erroneous belief systems which have held peoples apart from each other, instead of bringing the glorious unity Jesus prayed for in the garden of Gethsemane and the community He recreated in His finished work on the Cross. The gospel is Good News! And every believer is commissioned by Jesus to carry it to all peoples. To argue with this truth, is to argue with God Himself. Thank you, Dr. White, in bringing clarity and dispersing confusion.

—Reverend Shelley Christian, Christ The Answer International Ministries, Saskatoon (ctaim.org), Saskatchewan, Canada

The Birth that Counts speaks to an important issue. As a minister to native communities, I believe every obstacle to laborers coming into these harvest fields must be torn down. This includes confusion over the spiritual authority to preach the gospel. I believe Dr. Velma White gives a clear, biblical argument for receiving our authority from God first. If earthly authorities opposed Jesus, there is no reason to believe they will not oppose us. Yet, Jesus and the disciples continued to carry the gospel to every creature regardless of opposition. We too need to move out in that authority, not in arrogance but in humble obedience. I have always been impressed by Abraham who, when he was called by God, moved into Canaan, pastured his animals and even waged war all under the authority of God's call. We too need have the grace not to back down but to move in and take the land for the kingdom of God and may this book help us to do just that!

—Pastor Larry Keegstra, Living Water Ministries, Executive Director Camp Living Water, Vanderhoof B.C., Canada

The Birth that Counts is an important read for all who are engaged in cross-cultural ministry. Dr. White leaves no stone unturned as she unveils current "Christian trends" specific among her First Nations people that are hindering and tainting the message of the Gospel of Jesus Christ. Her findings, however, are relevant to all people groups everywhere. Such views as "Jurisdictional Authority," and "Regional Gatekeepers" are several of the important issues she discusses while pointing out solutions through Christ that brings harmony and unity rather than division and exclusivity. Dr. Velma White clearly illustrates that the Gospel message is not a social or tribal Gospel. It transcends all cultures. She builds her discussion on a revelation of Jesus Christ who alone is the core of our value and belief system. From this foundation she covers the essentials for a powerful fruitful ministry to restore and heal broken lives across every culture. You will be both inspired and informed through this timely work.

—Reverend Marie Brown, Marie Brown Ministries, North Carolina, USA

Dr. White presents her case clearly, concisely and practically. Her approach is based on eternal biblical truth and not current fads or trends which quickly lose relevance. The reader will enjoy this honest exploration of practices and influences that have hindered the growth of the Church and the spread of the Gospel, and appreciate the application of God's redemptive plan to solve these dilemmas.

—Dr. Chyanna Mull-Anthony, Pastor, International Gospel Center (www.IGCenter.org), Vice-President, Osborn Ministries, Int'l. (www.Osborn.org), Tulsa OK, USA

Dr. Velma White has a vision to see all people everywhere find their identity in Christ as they receive the Gospel. She gives voice to the need for each one to rise up in their God-given destinies and calling. Dr. White also believes this cannot be achieved without unity in the Body of Christ. Her book, The Birth That Counts deals with all three of these points. It is a "must read" book.

—Reverend Kathy Ageton, Kathy Ageton
Ministries, Sioux Falls South Dakota, USA

CONTENTS

ACKNOWLEDGMENTS

M y coworker and dear friend, Rev. Kathy Ageton.
My spiritual mentor, Bishop LaDonna Osborn.

Other Friends and Colleagues:

Gerald and Brenda Klosse and all who are part of their Friends Group.
Reverends Jim and Shelley Christian, founders of Christ The Answer
    International Ministries.
Dr. Chyanna Mull-Anthony, Senior Pastor at International Gospel
    Center.
Rev. Marie Brown at Marie Brown Ministries.
Rev. Susie Eichner, missionary sent from Abundant Life Ministries.
Pastor's Len and Sue Pawluski and their church family of the
    Dixonville Community Church.
Pastor Larry Keegstra at Camp Living Water.
Barnabas Ministries Church Fellowship.
Living Branches Community Church
My dear sister, Violet M. L. Ross.

Thank you all for your continuous insight, love, prayers, support, encouragement, and inspiration.

FOREWORD

Throughout history, God has chosen men and women to be his voice of hope, healing, and transformation. Dr. Velma White is one of those voices. She amplifies the loving voice of God among people groups that are too often neglected by Christian mission or relegated as outside the popular field of Gospel ministry.

As a citizen of the Cree Nation in Canada (often referred to as one of the First Nations), Dr. White is personally, intellectually, and spiritually qualified to address the vital needs of her people. She does not create a unique context for Christian mission among the native tribes of North America; rather, she adopts a broad biblical view of the issues and the solution that the Gospel of Jesus Christ brings.

As you read the pages that follow, expect to enter a world that demands your understanding and your response. You will discover how the eternal plan of God for his human creation applies to the cultural, historical, and traditional lifestyles of the native North American tribes. These represent global people groups that need the liberating and transforming truth of Jesus Christ. Regardless your mission field, this book will help you bring solution that lasts through your influence and ministry.

Personal identities of nationality, tribal origin, ethnicity, religion, political platform, skin color, gender, etc. increasingly tend to divide people. Christ comes through his glorious Gospel and restores

13

unity and harmony. Discover this profound truth as you grasp *The Birth that Counts.*

LaDonna Osborn, D. Min.
osborn.org
President, Osborn Ministries International
Bishop, International Gospel
Fellowship of Churches and Ministries
Founder, Women's International Network

INTRODUCTION

Biblical equality means equal opportunity and spiritual authority for all believers in Christ who have experienced spiritual new birth. Through faith in him, men and women are born again.[1] Therefore, spiritual authority is based upon the birth that counts; All believers, no matter their ethnic background, gender, or natural birth origin must rely solely upon the work of Christ in his death, burial, and resurrection.

Today, many preachers claim that our natural birth origin gives believers jurisdiction, "spiritual rank" over their geographical districts. The author of this book has termed this notion a "spiritual jurisdiction view." In this book, we will reveal from scripture that it is our spiritual birth—our being born again—that is the essence of who we are as believers. Our spiritual birth is our redeemed identity, and by this, we can confidently walk in our spiritual authority in his name.

It has been proven that the teaching of the truths of redemption produces biblical equality and Christian unity as this also removes strongholds of discriminatory mindsets. This volume will outline the following: The importance of being born again; our redeemed status; being included in his covenant; our privilege in prayer; the proper spiritual clothing—our identity in Christ; ministering everywhere in his name, and a conclusion that states the priority fact of the message of the Gospel.

---

[1] John 3:3–8

After years of ministry, the author has come across conflicting views regarding the significance of our natural birth (racial, birth origin, or gender) in contrast to our spiritual authority in Christ that we have as believers. In particular, this previous view has singled out Indigenous believers as having a singularized role in the kingdom of God. This also includes the notion that the natural birth of these believers attributes to them "extra" spiritual rank and privilege within the geographical locales in which they are born, allocating them as "gatekeepers" or "host people (we will continue to discuss these terms throughout this thesis)."

"Gatekeepers" then defined are those individuals who are from a community holding the right or authority toward visitors to grant permission for visitors to begin to do Christian ministry. For the Christian believer, the gate keepers do not necessarily need to be one of political authority; rather, it is allotted to the individual whose natural birth is from that area. This phrase, *gatekeeper*, has been commonly used in charismatic Christian circles among those who both misinterpret and misapply where spiritual authority is based. The belief then is that outsiders (or visitors) do not have adequate spiritual authority to minister to their indigenous people. Only local, natural born Christian believers can minister to their own people unless an identified "gatekeeper" invites them in.

The phrase "host people" is a common cultural term used among many non-Christian Indigenous gatherings and has become adopted in the charismatic Christian stream. Therefore, both phrases, "gatekeeper" and "host people" are commonly interlinked in light of the "spiritual jurisdiction view." The writer has given special attention to this notion about the "gatekeeper" in the chapter "The Gospel of Peace."

It is the author's belief that according to scripture, this view is not in harmony with biblical equality in the Great Commission given by Jesus Christ to his followers. The unfortunate consequence of the "spiritual jurisdiction view" has engendered further discrimination in Christian ministry within the Body of Christ. When believers accept this view, they disallow ministers of the Gospel who are not of their race, including those not of their tribe or natural birth origin. Those rejected by these Indigenous believers have been hindered in carrying out the mission in these places to which God has called them.

As discriminatory views are being addressed, certain terms will be used in this thesis: Indigenous, Native, First Nations, Aboriginal; interwoven with race, tribal, natural birth, origin of birth, locale as pertaining to tribal peoples and also including the term *gender*.

The objective of this study is to clarify a proper understanding of true spiritual authority through scripture and credible research. This investigation determines whether or not a person's natural birth (origin of birth) allocates individual believers' exclusive jurisdiction apart from those who are not from their respective land. The author emphasizes that for all believers, it is our spiritual rebirth in Christ— the birth that counts—that establishes the true basis for our spiritual authority.

We are investigating the following: a believer's identity in Christ in light of redemption and how that identity applies to our spiritual authority. We will observe how Jesus dealt with sectarianism among believers and also how the Apostle Paul dealt with similar issues.

Through these and other discussions, this review intends to assist the reader in reconsidering true biblical equality, Christian, unity and the Body of Christ's mission in the world. Additionally, the author brings into focus the goals that are inherent within the Gospel and the empowerment of the Holy Spirit. The author also seeks to help the reader to reconsider their own biases so that they can gain a new confidence in their new birth status in Christ.

SPIRITUAL
JURISDICTION VIEW

R acial discrimination in the Body of Christ between Indigenous and non-Indigenous believers has increased due to an erroneously held view. The belief held suggests that those who are not of their birth origin or race have insufficient spiritual authority to minister to the Indigenous people. In turn, they repudiate these "outsiders." This has caused great hindrance for the productive work of the Gospel in places to which God has called these "outsiders." They are unable to minister in these locations because of the antagonism coming from those misled believers who embrace this opinion.

By contrast, several non-Native ministers desire to show respect and honor toward their Native brothers and sisters in Christ. The author appreciates the effort on the part of those non-Native ministers who genuinely care for their Native brothers and sisters in Christ as they attempt to reach out to them.

Other Native ministers seek the same objective. Both seek to bridge the gapping racial divide. This dynamic has swelled the "spiritual jurisdiction view" by integrating culturally relevant approaches among the Native mission fields in order to gain acceptance. With the intention of facilitating a cultural ceremonial welcome, it is believed that through this act, spiritual authority will have been "transferred" from the "gatekeeper" or "host people"—the local Native believers.

It has become faddish to participate in this type of official ceremonial welcoming. Upon this, a belief fixates that spiritual authority has been conveyed through those local participants of the ceremony. Even with this fashion, in spite of this accepted idea, those who believe they hold the power to "transfer" this spiritual authority choose not to officially welcome outsiders due to their own biases. The barrier still remains; racism and discrimination are not resolved.

In either case, the notion about spiritual authority has been misapplied through the practice of this type of formal ritual as initiated by local participants. However practical this approach may seem, the author believes that this kind of protocol has been over-spiritualized (more on this will be discussed in the chapter, "Our Redeemed Status.")

Scripturally, the "spiritual jurisdiction view" contradicts the purpose of the Great Commission where Jesus commands his followers to make disciples of all nations.[2] This erroneous teaching prevents God's plan of biblical equality and Christian unity among his redeemed community. We must reconsider our approach to Christian ministry to become reacquainted with the principles taught by Christ. These principles embodied by the first century church illustrate the standards for all believers which must continue to be applied today.

This discussion surfaces several questions: In light of our spiritual authority in Christ, what role does our biological DNA have to do with our spiritual authority? If this is of significance, do we see Jesus, as well as the apostles, teaching on this matter? Why has the result of this view caused more discrimination and uncertainty among those who accept it? These questions will be answered in the sections following.

In part, the writer agrees with the necessity for First Nation believers to rise up in their God-given identity and role as this is prerequisite to the fulfilment of the Great Commission that all nations should be reached with the Gospel. The scriptures teach us that when one member of the Body of Christ suffers, we suffer with them, that we also rejoice when one member is being honored; as believers, we are to honor one another in the dignity and equality we each have received in Christ.[3]

---

[2] Matthew 28:19
[3] Romans 12:20–26

However, their arising (including any other culture) does not include the resurgence of ungodly ceremonies and cultural traditions which have no biblical roots. This form of syncretism confuses the biblical concept about redemption of all nations and insinuates that the individual and all their culture, be it biblical or not, are allowed full expression.

The Bible does not endorse this mixture. This amalgamation integrates within the "spiritual jurisdiction view" as it also results in the exclusion of non-Native believers who are called to minister to Native people. In the Great Commission, we are called to work together but not at the expense of integrating ungodly ceremonies with Christian faith nor the participation of it.

We need to understand that Indigenous people are in a time of transition where a pluralistic philosophy has become the norm. We also understand from history about the colonization of the Indigenous people for governmental control of them. Native people were stripped of everything they were, many injustices occurred, including the negative impact of the residential school era. The 1970s brought in centralized efforts to revitalize their language, cultural and religious traditions, as they also feel justified in their aspiration to recover what they feel they lost. It is a quest for their lost identity.

For those Native believers in Christ who begin to understand their true identity in Christ, they come to discover through God's Word how unnecessary it is to blend their former Native cultural traditions and beliefs with Christian teachings. They discover that truths of Christ's substitutionary work are sufficient. They have come to find their security in the finished work of Christ. Naturally, their attention about who they are becomes centered on Christ.

The author does not assume this about these individuals, but rather has witnessed this upon numerous occasions in many lives. As an Indigenous believer seeking redemption and spiritual healing, the writer had not yet realized that in Christ, her true identity—being made in the image of God—was already redeemed.

Upon this enlightenment, the writer also discontinued syncretistic practices and pursued biblical truth. The writer began to discover from scripture what it means to identify with Christ and to also find her value in the redemption that was made at Christ's substitutionary work.

In fairness to some of these who seek to inspire Native believers to arise in their calling, they intend to express acceptance of them in Christian ministry for the sake of Christian unity. This is done by misinterpreting scripture by sharing "revelations" they perceive and speak forth "prophetically" as they are concerned for Native people. However, because many Indigenous people still resent non-Natives as they receive this kind of speech, in turn, they are empowered negatively. What forms among these believers is an "us and them" mentality.

This also is not an assumption on the part of the author. Rather, through the last several years, this has been witnessed firsthand in the way some of these misled Indigenous believers have treated those not of their race, also including how non-Natives treat Indigenous believers. This is called discrimination. The "spiritual jurisdiction view" teaching has not solved the problem of racism; instead, it has only fostered it. This should never be experienced in the Body of Christ.

One more note of interest, among Native tribes, there are many who are of an animistic worldview within their own culture and religion. This influence how they interpret their way of life, culture, traditions, customs, and spirituality. Among many of these tribes, a tribal and hierarchical system is given precedence, even among Native Christian circles who are untaught in the truths of redemption. A colleague in ministry shared his experience:

> The tribal people we have been ministering to in this region, believe that certain clan members cannot speak in regions not of their own because they are from a different clan. They believe that a clan leader must welcome them and grant them authority to address their clan before they can minister to them. Even the believers in Christ from these clans accept this as a part of divine order within Christian ministry. This hinders

an outsider's validity in ministering the gospel
to their people. I don't recall any of that being
taught from scripture.[4]

As a First Nations tribal member, the writer can also affirm that
Native people are prone to emphasize their tribal territory. By this,
they assume the position of being a "host people" and "gatekeepers"
having "original authority." This idea is already embedded into their
way of thinking culturally whether they are believers in Christ or not.

Consider these two firsthand experiences (names of communities and people remain anonymous):

> As I was travelling with a ministry team in a cer-
> tain region of Canada. Our leaders were non-na-
> tive while the remaining team represented three
> different Indigenous groups. The areas where
> we were holding Gospel outreach meetings were
> mainly Native communities. Through the years
> this ministry has maintained ongoing outreaches
> to this area with a variety of team members.
> Unfortunately, a certain false teaching made its
> way into this area as certain believers from this
> area began to accept this teaching. These believ-
> ers went ahead of the ministry team which I was
> a part of and began to discredit us, giving bad
> reports about us before we arrived. They believed
> they were right in doing what they did because
> we were not of their kind, therefore they justified
> their actions. Obviously, these believers were mis-
> led and the result of their activity only hindered
> the work of Gospel ministry to this unreached
> community.[5]

---

4   Interview via phone conference, December 23, 2017, Interviewee Confidential
5   Interview via email, March 14th, 2017, Interviewee Confidential

The second firsthand experience was relayed by a ministry colleague currently dealing with discriminating issues in Christian ministry:

> There has been a movement of late in the places we have ministered in Canada, that no longer seems to want "white" ministers in the North. Many of the places we have ministered now just surround themselves with First Nations ministers. While we celebrate this as wonderful in many ways...we also know that the Lord does not look on the outward appearance, but the heart...and we know that the message of reconciliation and restoration in Christ is NOT being heard in many of these areas. The teenagers are still destroying themselves on so many of the reserves. (name disclosed) and I want God's perfect plan...and we still believe we are called to all points North and South in Canada. Thank you for agreeing with us for barricades blocking the gospel to bust wide open.[6]

These are two of many unfortunate experiences where this discrimination is perpetrated due to this trendy yet erroneous teaching by both non-Native or native ministers. Ironically, Native ministers are also facing this rejection because they are not of another tribal group and/or clan. These unfortunate incidences are taking place in the communities of those believers who attend such gatherings that teach the "spiritual jurisdiction view." The outcomes breed contempt, exclusion, and inequality.

The author concludes that only a proper understanding of redemption will eradicate this kind of thinking and renews one's mind toward biblical equality. This review not only exposes the prob-

---

[6] Interview via email, October 5th, 2017, Interviewee Confidential

lem but presents the biblical view by setting forth clear evidence, a true understanding of biblical equality, and our identity in Christ through the lens of redemption. Thorough research from scripture including numerous valid resources have been given in view of true spiritual authority our identity in Christ, biblical equality, and Christian unity through the lens of biblical redemption.

The Birth that Counts will cause readers to renew their confidence in who they are in Christ. It will also eradicate prejudice and discrimination which seems to be a stronghold in the minds of untaught and misled believers. It will enable readers to honor and value other Christian workers.

Appreciating what numerous authors have written on the topic of who we are in Christ and biblical equality, the writer intends to apply these truths in addressing this erroneous view. This study presents a clear argument that our spiritual birth is the birth that counts, therefore our origin of birth, race, or gender does not empower our position as believers with spiritual authority in fulfilling Christ's Great Commission. That through Christ, all believers have equal spiritual authority. All believers must rest solely upon the work of Christ in his death, burial, and resurrection for their position, purpose, and identity in living as a member of the Body of Christ.

This problem is significant when consequences are evident, such as further division in Christian ministry within the Body of Christ. The priority of proper teaching from scripture on this subject demands our attention. Therefore, an investigation from scripture regarding the matter is necessary to bring about biblical unity and to also understand biblical equality through the scope of redemption.

The writer believes it is necessary to examine by scripture *The Birth that Counts* in response to the problem and to bring solution to this problem. In this book, we have presented: What is true spiritual authority? An understanding that redemption of all people in light of the new covenant exposes the lies of discrimination, and it also refocuses on true biblical equality, spiritual authority, and Christian unity.

1

The Importance of Being Born Again

Jesus answered and said to him,
"Most assuredly, I say to you, unless one is born
again, he cannot see the kingdom of God"

—John 3:3, NKJV

Jesus was in conversation with Nicodemus. Who was Nicodemus? He was a man who was a Pharisee holding a position as part of the Sanhedrin, the Jewish council. The Sanhedrin were a very important sect in the Jewish society of Nicodemus' day who also kept the Roman government informed in matters pertaining to Judaism and Jewish customs.[7]

Nicodemus would have understood that his people were the chosen people whom God had ordained to represent him to the world of coming to God his way. They had been given the law through Moses whom God had revealed his glory to. He also would have recognized why his people were no longer in power as a kingdom due the disobedience of their forefathers thereby bringing judgement upon their people as a whole. They did not continue in his covenant.

---

[7] Cross, John R. *By This Name*, Copyright © 2010 by GoodSeed International, Electronic Edition 2, Publisher: GoodSeed International, Olds, Alberta, Canada, Chapter 11, Section 3

Four hundred years had passed since the prophecy of Malachi, and no fresh revelation from God had come. By this time in their history, Israel was subjected to the Roman regime with Caesar as ruler.

It seems at this time, this generation had begun to return to the Lord and to the Word of God, namely the Torah. It would be through the use of the synagogues where they would study the laws of Moses, the psalms, and the prophets. The Jewish temple had been reconstructed, and the sacrificial system was reinstituted with the order of priests as shown in the books of Moses.

Nicodemus had given his life to serve God. As a faithful follower of the covenant, we can assume his zeal for the righteousness of God not only for his life, but also for his people to be what God had called them to be. He would have also known the prophecies of the coming Deliverer—the Messiah—whom God promised to send from the time of Adam and Eve. However, Nicodemus did not understand the spiritual kingdom—the kingdom of God. The kingdom of God was not like any earthly kingdom, not even of his own nation.

Let's look again at the words of Jesus: "Unless one is born again, he cannot see the kingdom of God" (John 3:3, NKJV). He uses a word of stipulation; unless, in other words, if this does not happen or if this condition is not met, it is impossible to see the kingdom of God. Being born again is not a mere suggestion as though there were another means to enter the kingdom of God. Kenneth E. Hagin wrote:

> It doesn't matter how well-educated man becomes, how many degrees he has at the end of his name, how many dollars he has, how good a social worker he is, nor how religious he is—man cannot stand in the presence of God. His nature is wrong. Man is lost today, not because of what he does—but because of what he is. (What he does is the result of what he is). Man needs life from God, because he is spiritually dead.[8]

---

[8] Hagin, Kenneth E., *The New Birth*, Chapter 2, electronic edition, copyright©1975 RHEMA Bible Church, aka Kenneth Hagin Ministries, Inc. All

Jesus saw Nicodemus' spiritual blindness to the importance of how one can attain the righteousness of God. For without the righteousness of God, none could be in his presence. He wanted him to understand that acceptability in the kingdom of God is not found upon the reliance of one's own righteousness. He wanted him to see that his natural birth right did not give him this kind of righteousness; neither did it give him right to enter the kingdom of God.

John R. Cross wrote:

> But Jesus was concerned about something different—Nicodemus' soul. He knew Nicodemus thought he was good enough-for-God—that he was trusting in His own goodness because he kept the Law of Moses meticulously. He also knew that Nicodemus prided himself in being part of the Chosen People... Jesus knew that Nicodemus was trusting in his Jewish ancestry to make himself acceptable to God. Jesus wanted to show him that his faith was placed in the wrong birth. So, Jesus told him, 'Ye must be born again.'[9]

Today, this truth remains the same. Our own righteousness does not make us fit to stand in the presence of God. We need God's righteousness. Being born in the natural as a Jew would not give privilege over others who were not. If one were truly concerned how he or she could see the kingdom of God, then one would have to understand what is necessary in order for them to have that right. We need the righteousness of God—we must be born again. We then must ask: How do we acquire his righteousness? How is this possi-

---

[9] Cross, John R. *By This Name,* Copyright © 2010 by GoodSeed International, Publisher: GoodSeed International, Olds, Alberta, Canada, pg. 242

ble? Nicodemus reasoned the concept of being born again with a question:

> How can a man be born again when he is old?
> Can he enter a second time into his mother's
> womb and be born? (John 3:4, NKJV)

As logical as that question may have been, Nicodemus was missing the point. Seeing the kingdom of God had nothing to do with the natural means of this life. His natural birth did not make him worthy. He trusted in his natural birth. After all, he was born of the chosen people.

However, even though this was true, being born of the chosen people, he still needed to be born again.

What was Jesus saying? As far as heaven is concerned, there are two categories of humans: those who have been born once, and those who have been born twice. If any person has not been born again, they simply will not see the kingdom of God. However, if anyone has been born again, they will see his kingdom. Nicodemus placed his confidence in the wrong birth. He was certain that his natural birth would assure him a place in the kingdom of God.

Being a religious ruler of his people, who were the chosen people, caused him to believe he was worthy of the kingdom of God. T. L. Osborn writes on *How to be Born Again*:

> The miracle of the new birth is experienced when
> one accepts Christ into his or her heart by faith.
> This miracle does not take place by accepting a
> religion; it is engendered in a person when they
> accept the Christ-Life—not a philosophy but
> a person, not a liturgy but a life, not a religion
> but a reality, not by sharing a ceremony, but by
> becoming a new creation.[10]

---

[10] Osborn, T. L. *How to Be Born Again*, Copyright ©2002 by LaDonna C. Osborn, Publishers: Osborn Publishers, Tulsa, OK, 74102, pg. 48

We must understand that being born again does not mean that one is joining a different religion, denomination, or culture. Those who have been born again are those who have received his righteousness through their acceptance of Jesus as Lord and Savior alone. These are those who have not placed their confidence in themselves or in their natural birth. They are also those who identify with the one who God sent and rely upon him for salvation. Believing and receiving Jesus is what brings a person in right standing with God. In view of the fact that Jesus was sent from God, he is able to state the conditional spiritual law for all to see and enter the kingdom of God.

Reverend Shelley Christian shared that as born-again believers, we carry a new type of DNA:

> Christianity is not a religion. To be a believer in Jesus Christ is to enter into a Family. The Family of God Himself. We become citizens of heaven and representatives of God. We are given the amazing purpose of reproducing His image on the earth... Natural children bear their parents DNA. When we are born again as God's offspring, created in His image and in His likeness, we carry His spiritual DNA (Divine Nature Activated).[11]

This truth helps us to realize that the born-again experience is that of a supernatural occurrence within the life of the one who confesses and repents of their sins and accepts Christ as their Lord and Savior. "But as many as received him, to them He gave the right to become the children of God, to those who believe in His name" (John 1:12, NKJV). We are given this right as we have become born again, thereby being made a part of the spiritual family of God. We are then made citizens of heaven and are joined to the Body of Christ.

---

[11] Christian, Shelley, "Spirit, Soul and Body Wholeness," Seminar notes at NTOMI Discipleship Bible School, Ft. Providence, NT, November 18–11, 2013, pg. 3

Not a new concept, but a fundamental one; although for most believers, each one realizes the importance of being born again. The author is not attempting to add new knowledge to this fundamental truth but to reemphasize this crucial part in order to establish that without this first step, we have no standing with God.

Therefore, without being born again, we have no authority over the devil either. If we are not born again, we are still dead in our sins and remain under the rule of Satan, and this is true for all who are born into this world. It is only until we individually are born again that we come out from under the rule of Satan. Satan does not fear the child of God because of their natural birth but because that individual has become and knows they are a child of God.

Our spiritual confidence is no longer centered on the self-made image we formed for ourselves, even if it was what we have always known in this world. In his hour of trial, Jesus said to Pilate, "My kingdom is not of this world..." (John 18:36a).

Therefore, those who desire to see and enter the kingdom of heaven cannot do so through the means of the natural orders of this world. Seeing and entering the kingdom of heaven is based only upon accepting Jesus as our only means of salvation and receiving his righteousness. Jesus is the foundation of who we are as believers. He is our identification in the new birth. It was crucial that Nicodemus hear Jesus say to him that he must be born again, meaning that he could not rely upon his natural birth or his own means of good works. This truth has not changed for our generation today.

This truth continues to remain the same as we progress in our walk with Christ. Spiritual authority, rights, or privileges within the kingdom of God cannot be acquired through any other means of this earth, except that we are first born again. There is no greater revelation outside of this truth. Our former experiences, education, careers, status, including our natural birth culture, tribe or race, and gender does not earn us the right to the kingdom of God. These may have its merit for the systems of this world as preference, but they are trivial, having no value or worth in matters of our acceptance into the kingdom of God. Two Jewish writers, McIntosh and Twyman, gave these comments on the aspect of being born again:

> Spiritual birth, true religion, is not confined, as you Jews suppose, to one tribe or family. It is as free as air, and the kingdom of God, which you expect to a national thing, will spread over the earth as that does, without any regard to the boundaries of nations and kindred's. Its empire is the soul, everywhere free, everyone capable of receiving it, not more in those whose material bodies have descended from Abraham than those who have never heard of his name.[12]

The aspect of the spiritual birth—our being born again—is therefore imperative for believers to understand and never lose sight of. For it is from this place that all believers can rest assured having confidence in their spiritual new birth identity in Christ. This powerful truth warrants all believers equivalent significance in the kingdom of God.

---

[12] McIntosh & Twyman, Drs., *The Archko Volume*, Translated by Drs. McIntosh & Twyman of the Antiquarian Lodge, Genoa Italy, Unabridged Edition, copyright©1975 by Keats Publishing, Inc. Keats Publishing, Inc, 212 Elm Street, New Canaan, Connecticut 06840 USA

2

Our Redeemed Status

An Observation: Over-Spiritualization of Protocol

The writer has heard in person from several Christian platforms and as well from individual believers in Christ state a position that Christian ministry is conditional to the locale to which a believer is from, and in that place, they hold spiritual authority. This modern theology assumes that the natural birthplace to where an individual believer was born qualifies them additional spiritual authority in that location. In other cases, some believers suppose that because they were a descendant from another country, they could exercise an "elite" spiritual authority in that territory.

However, the assumed relevance becomes blurred when these individuals travel to minister in other places where none of their descendants came from. Questions then surface: Were they out of order? Since they are not from there and if they believe the former claim, then why go to other regions in which they have no tie to their ancestors?

This has brought confusion as to where our spiritual authority is founded. The application of this teaching seemed to be rather superficial and insubstantial. Whenever the writer would question this claim, which those of this view believed, they would give this rationale or rather justified answer, "We need to be welcomed by the host people. That is how we will be given spiritual authority to minister in their regions."[13] This relates to protocol within a system where these conventions have been precedent.

Since the writer comes from a tribal people group, the writer is prone to understand protocol. Protocol varies in many places. It is regarded that when protocol is used, authorization is granted by the one who introduces the visitor to the group who is being addressed. The custom of protocol in many places is crucial. Therefore, protocol in and of itself is a valued practice for both parties. It is considered that by using protocol, the group perceives that the leader knows the individual. Therefore, by introduction and acknowledgement of the foreigner, they will have validated their presence among them.

Modern theology in light of the "spiritual jurisdiction view" has also over spiritualized the practice of protocol. It is believed that because the person from a certain district occupies spiritual authority over that region, this person bears the right to "transfer" that spiritual authority to the visitor, thereby qualifying the visiting ministry. It is believed, even feared, that God's blessing will not be released in that region if this spiritual protocol does not take place.[14]

This has incited a misapplication about spiritual authority, which insinuates that these individuals are a source of power unto themselves, alluding to them the ability to transfer their spiritual authority. This provokes this question: Is this not the kind of ideology, which onsets the hierarchy system implemented within the mid-age church, to which the dark ages began?

Whenever this trendy view was brought to her attention, the writer would be left with the sense of inadequacy and exclusion. As at other times, the writer sensed that her ego had been stroked. In the meantime, an increasing awareness of many genuine Christian ministries have been excluded in places where this ideology is accepted, and more honest questions arise: What about those who I believe I am called to work with who are not of the descent of my people? Do they now have no spiritual authority in these places? Are they out of

---

[13] Dialogue with interviewee, April 14th, 2015, Interviewee confidential
[14] Dialogue with interviewee, February 28th, 2018, Interviewee confidential

order when they go to regions they know that God has called them to which they are not born of?

More questions stir: Why would God call you to a region where you are not from or at least where your ancestors are not from after all? And since you are not from there, you have no spiritual authority? It makes one wonder: Why then did Jesus go to Samaria? Why did Paul go to the gentiles? Why did the first believers leave Jerusalem at all?

In fact, as we study the time of the first century church in the book of Acts, we find that the places where they took the message of the Gospel did not have a Gospel light, meaning no one (a gatekeeper) was there to welcome them to transfer their authority to those apostles who came to their region, authorizing them to preach the Gospel in order to be effective.

As we read their account, we find clues that the only indication to which the apostles had was a witness of the Holy Spirit. They knew Jesus had already granted them authority to preach the Gospel and do the works of the kingdom; they also knew that he was sending them into all the world. We see in their account no indication in Jesus's commissioning that they were to wait for protocol to be initiated by a certain "gatekeeper," nor do we see any implications that their authority will be effective because they were of that location. The only condition the Lord had given in order that his followers will have power to be witnesses was when they received the Holy Spirit into their lives.[15]

If the "spiritual jurisdiction view" was spot on that as believers, we have supplementary spiritual authority in the land of our ancestors, in addition, the writer then asks this question: What is the point of being born again?

---

[15] Matthew 28:18–20; Mark 16:15–18; Acts 1:8

Spiritual Authority Based Upon Our Spiritual Birth

Observing Colossians 2:6, "As you therefore have received Christ Jesus the Lord, so walk in him," in the same way, we all must receive Christ Jesus; we are exhorted to walk in that manner. That is, we relied upon him alone to save us from our sins. It is therefore required that we also rely upon him to walk in his righteousness and the authority he has given us. Out of curiosity, the writer has searched the scriptures for understanding and, like Nicodemus, inquired of the Lord to reveal truth within the scriptures to see if this modern theological view, "spiritual authority based on our natural birth teaching," was in keeping with biblical truth. This question was brought forth: Was it true that I, as a believer, had more spiritual authority in my native land than other believers who were not born of my descent?

As the writer has researched the scriptures, looking for the slightest possibility, the writer has found this claim about the "spiritual jurisdiction view" to be heretical. It is not in harmony with biblical truth and biblical equality. The writer has also come to learn that as believers, our spiritual authority is based upon our spiritual birth. Our spiritual authority is not dependent upon anything we are in the natural. It may be so that certain personalities tend to have a measure of influence among their own kind, but it is not from this source to which spiritual authority rests.

As discussed earlier, Jesus's conversation with Nicodemus that his right to enter the kingdom of God was conditional to his spiritual birth—that he must be born again.

Paul wrote of our position in heavenly places in Christ Jesus:

> But God, who is rich in mercy, because of His great love with which He loved us, even when we were dead in trespasses, made us alive together with Christ (by grace you have been saved), and raised us up together, and made us sit together in the heavenly places in Christ Jesus.

> Now, therefore, you are no longer strang-
> ers and foreigners, but fellow citizens with the
> saints and members of the household of God.
> (Ephesians 2:4–6,19, NKJV)

This speaks of our citizenship in heaven which abrogates any postulation about our natural birth identity as to our competency to walk in the spiritual authority of the kingdom of heaven. Protocol may help in the natural as a practical means, but it has no additional dynamic in the spiritual. Without any citizenship in heaven, there is no legitimate spiritual authority available to us. In reality, without being born again, we are still under Satan's rule. Without being born again, we remain spiritually dead in our sins. Our natural birth privilege that we feel we possess is not able to change our spiritually depraved condition. It cannot improve it. In reality, we are in need of a spiritual rebirth. Our reception of Christ makes this possible, and through this, we are born again by faith in him.

When we start to recognize that in Christ we are made citizens of the kingdom of heaven, this understanding produces confidence to utilize the rights and privileges of the kingdom. It is based within our redeemed status as a born-again child of God. As our lives are in submission to his will and under his direction, he will send us forth with the power invested in his name to represent Christ in this world. With this in mind, these words of Paul become even more perceptible:

> Now then, we are ambassadors for Christ, as
> though God were pleading through us: we implore
> you on Christ's behalf, be reconciled to God. (2
> Corinthians 5:20)

An ambassador is one who is first of all a citizen of the country, which they represent. This ambassador knows the values which the nation's laws are formulated and its countries agenda. An ambassador understands that the words that they are to speak are those of the ruler of the nation they represent. They are conscious that they do not represent themselves or speak of their own words. These principles of ambassadorship apply to believers of Christ everywhere.

Simply, our being sent is not about us. It is about the kingdom of heaven. Our code of conduct is centered on who we are in Christ as his ambassadors. We must realize that we been given the use of his name and a message to proclaim. This a sacred charge, "But as we have been approved by God to be entrusted with the gospel..." (1 Thessalonians 2:4a, NKJV).

Therefore, it is vital that as believers in Christ, we must become intimately acquainted with our identity in Christ as a citizen of heaven. We must begin to walk in the liberating reality of our redeemed status. We must learn to be identified with him and no longer seek importance within the appraises of this world. Paul wrote plainly to the Philippian believers:

> For we are the circumcision, who worship God
> in the Spirit, rejoice in Christ Jesus, and have no
> confidence in the flesh. (Philippians 3:3)

As one who had many credentials, Paul truly walked in the revelation of his identity in Christ, and as a result, he walked in the authority of Christ. He understood that his spiritual authority and spiritual identity had nothing to do with his earthly accomplishments or his natural birth.[16] His confidence was not in the flesh (or plainly put, the self-made man he had become prior to his conversion).

Our Heavenly Citizenship—Our Redeemed Status

In many tribal cultures, one is recognized according to the clan they represent. Others adhere to a caste system. In some places, one is given preference according to their status by the amount of wealth their families hold. It is important to recognize that these types of attributes are a standard of the world system apart from true

---

[16] Philippians 3:14–15

Christian values, and they are also opposite in attitudes to that of the kingdom of heaven.

Let's read again Ephesians 2:19:

> Now, therefore, you are no longer strangers and foreigners, but fellow citizens with the saints and members of the household of God. (Ephesians 2:19, NKJV)

When one is born into a country, they are registered as a citizen of that country. As a result, a government birth certificate has been issued to prove that individual as having been born of that country and is a legal citizen of that nation. This principle applies to born-again believers of Jesus Christ. The book of Revelations speaks of this spiritual registration, "And anyone not found written in the Book of Life was cast into the lake of fire" (Revelations 20:15, NKJV).

"Anyone not found written" denotes an unmet requirement. It is more than mandatory that we become born again while we have lived our lives on this earth. If we physically die before having had this born-again experience, we will not be granted entrance to the kingdom of God. The consequences are eternal based on each individual's choice to believe or not believe the Gospel. For those who believe, repent, and receive the Gospel of Jesus, their names are written in heaven. These are also those who have become born again—made a citizen of heaven.

How critical it is that we as believers understand that within Christianity, no matter where we live, we must become conscious about which citizenship or status matters most. As believers in Christ, we have been born again. Born again into what? We are born again into the very kingdom of heaven, thereby making us citizens of heaven. Our spiritual status has been changed—we are redeemed from slavery to sin. This spiritual status positions all believers in the realm of being seated in heavenly places in Christ, thereby making us equal with one another regardless of our natural condition.

As citizens of the kingdom of heaven, this is now our new identity. Although we live in this earth in the flesh, we are no longer of this earth. We now have a new home, a spiritual home. The grave is not our final destination. We are citizens of heaven with the millions and millions of born-again believers in Christ. As far as God is concerned, his kingdom is our source of identity. The kingdom of heaven is our eternal home. This is our inheritance, our place of representation, and position of who we are. We are children of the most-high God—citizens of heaven.

As believers, we no longer live our lives by the merits of this world, but rather, we now live by the values of the kingdom of God, "[t]he life that I now live, I live by the faith of the Son of God…" (Galatians 2:20). This brings about identification with his kingdom as we discover through his Word its virtues and values. Ultimately, an intimate relationship with him is formed. Although we live in the flesh in this world, our mindsets transform to the attitudes of Christ. We are conformed to his image.

We read in Ephesians 2:19 about being a fellow citizen. The word *citizen* from *Strong's*: "a native of the same town."[17]

Spiritually, we are natives of heaven. "For our citizenship is in heaven" (Philippians 3:20, NKJV). We are joined in equality and community with all believers of Christ, being brought into heavens spiritual family. In Christ, we have a commonality that surpasses restrictions of jurisdiction, racial, tribal, gender, age, or status barriers which this world struggles with. In Christ, we are equally significant.

Through Christ, we have a common hope that cannot be destroyed. We have a source of joy that no one can take away. We have life that is filled with dignity and purpose. As believers, we are of the royal family of God. Therefore, as believers in Christ, we have equality with one another. Due to our redeemed status in Christ, each of us are granted equal opportunity to do the works of the kingdom of heaven in his name.

---

[17] Strong's word number: g4847 "citizen": *Olive Tree Enhanced Strong's Dictionary* Copyright 1998-2017 Olive Tree Bible Study Software

3

Biblical Equality

E quality defined: the state of being equal, especially in status, rights, or opportunities.[18]

As we break down this definition, we see how each defined part voices the virtues of Christian unity where biblical equality is perceived. We understand that the apostle Paul faced the challenge of dealing with issues of inequality as seen in his epistles, Romans being one of them, for example. "For we have previously charged both Jews and Greeks that they are all under sin" (Romans 3:9b, NKJV).

This was to address that his own race of people—the Jews— were no more righteous than non-Jews. Therefore, Jews and non-Jews were equally required to repent and believe the Gospel in order to acquire a right standing with God. In another epistle, "[t]hat the Gentiles should be fellow heirs, of the same body, and partakers of His promise in Christ through the gospel" (Ephesians 3:6, NKJV). In this letter, he indicates that Gentiles had equal opportunity in the promise of God in the same measure as did the Jews.

In his letter to the Galatians, "God shows no personal favoritism to man" (Galatians 2:6b, NKJV). He continues in Galatians 2:11–21 about an incident that took place regarding the apostle Peter's error in disassociating himself from non-Jews. Paul boldly rebuked him

---

[18] *Oxford Dictionary*, Copyright 1998, 2003, 2005, 2010, Oxford University Press, Great Clarendon Street, Oxford, pg. 591

for his hypocrisy. Peter should have known better; after all, it was he who received the vision from the Lord teaching him that all nations were now included in the Christian faith as we read in Acts chapters ten through eleven.

Paul was definitely well-acquainted with the issues of discrimination and inequality. Throughout his letters, he taught the truths of redemption which unveiled the new creation realities for all believers to grasp aspects of Christian equality as this prompts a natural maintaining of genuine Christian unity. This ought to be our example to follow.

How Biblical Equality Is Seen

The brief quote by Allan G Padgett, from the following article gives an insightful definition of biblical equality:

> Biblical equality is rooted and grounded in our Savior, Christ the Lord, and in his book. We have seen that biblical equality means human equality of all in the image of God; equal responsibility for all believers without regard to wealth, class, gender, or race; and mutual submission to one another in the name of Christ.[19]

Biblical equality begins to be applied when we start to embrace the truths of redemption as we perceive our new creation identity in Christ. Marie Brown shares her experience with the numerous cultures she has been among; her observations are well-stated:

> Traveling from one culture to another, I have often observed a feeling of superiority rise up between different groups of people. The only way

---

[19] Padgett, Alan G. "What Is Biblical Equality?" Website What Is Biblical Equality— Padgett.pdf, www.biblicalequality.org/index.php?option+com_docman&task= doc_download

bias and prejudice can be wiped out is through the Gospel of Jesus Christ. Sin produces this feeling of racial or cultural superiority, and its by-products are abuse, domination, and discrimination. This has never been God's way or His will. Unfortunately, this racial prejudice, ethnic bigotry and oppression has been often practiced in the name of God.

Paul wrote to the Galatian believers, "there is neither Jew nor Greek, there is neither slave nor free, there is neither male nor female; for you are all one in Christ Jesus" (Galatians 3:28, NKJV). This was written to help them understand their equal position before God and with each other as believers in Christ. It is necessary that biblical equality be taught and emphasized in order to guard against any forms of prejudice which the enemy would seek to sow seeds of contempt which hinders our fellowship with one another (see Appendix A).[20]

It is crucial for believers to recognize that our origin of birth, race, or gender in a sense is irrelevant to attaining our heavenly citizenship. It is due to that heavenly citizenship that we identify our place in the kingdom of God. It is vital that we begin to view all believers of various backgrounds within the Body of Christ in this light—that we are coequals.

We also learn that when those sent on a mission into lands not of their own, they are fulfilling the greater mandate of heaven. As believers and ministers, we have a new perspective. Our perspective in ministering the Gospel is not based on our natural identity but in our spiritual identity in Christ. Sarah Shin gives

---

[20] Brown, Marie, *God Has No Favorites*, Copyright © 2001 by H. Marie Brown, Publisher: Marie Brown Ministries, Inc. Tulsa, OK, 74170, pg. 46

this following insight on the matter of racial barriers in Christian ministry:

> Colorblindness says, "We're all the same." This mindset may be a well-meaning response to overt racism, but treating everyone as the same is different from treating everyone as equals. We are equal in the eyes of God, but we are not the same— we are different from each other in our experiences of culture, ethnicity, race, and injustice. Colorblindness unintentionally pretends like cultural differences and painful histories don't matter.
>
> In contrast, ethnicity-aware witness means that women and men of every ethnic background can humbly and boldly share about Jesus with people who don't look like them (instead of reaching primarily to those who share their culture).[21]

We are challenged to pursue reaching across any cultural barriers with the message of the Gospel. We are able to do so effectively when we begin to see past the skin color of an individual to the soul of the one in need of Christ as Savior. All cultural differences are to be settled at the foot of the cross. All human beings deserve to hear the Gospel with the love of Jesus. Ken Ham in his book, *One Race, One Blood*, states:

> We all need to treat every human being as our relative. We are of one blood. All of us are equal in value before our Creator God. Any descendant of Adam can be saved, because our mutual relative by blood (Jesus Christ) died and rose again. This

---

[21] Shin, Sarah, "Racial Difference Without Division, The Power of an Ethnicity-Honoring Witness." Sarah Shin, Theology & Spirituality, Christianity Today, November 14, 2017, http://www.chrisitianitytoday.org

is why the Gospel can and should be preached to all tribes and nations.[22]

There is a healthy balance of not ignoring the cultural customs and norms from which individuals are from or those who we are called to. We are to be aware and educated about the customs and traditions of the cultures to which we are sent without compromising our own biblical convictions. Our attaining of this information should not be to integrate non-biblical practices with biblical teachings. Not everyone agrees in terms of participation. However, it is beneficial to always walk in love without negating biblical principles. Efrem Smith gives the following insight:

> If there was ever a time for pastoral leadership with the ability to lead Christ-centered and multicultural communities, now is the time. The reason I say Christ-centered is because leading a multicultural congregation should not compromise biblical truth. Some churches in the United States of America and beyond have sacrificed biblical truth for the sake of becoming multicultural. This Christ-centeredness and belief in the authority and centrality of scripture ought to lead us to proclaiming truth, righteousness, evangelism, discipleship, and kingdom justice. A true commitment to Christ-centeredness in no way compromises the commitment to biblical truth, because the word of God is the beginning point for understanding the nature, words, and works of Christ. This ought to be the on-ramp to the next area, which is cross-cultural leadership.[23]

---

[22] Ham, Ken; A. Charles Ware. *One Race One Blood* (Kindle Locations 1263-1265). Master Books.

[23] Smith, Efram. "Pastors: God Calls Us to Cross-Cultural Ministry." https://sojo.net/articles/pastors-god-calls-us-cross-cultural-ministry

What these writers inform us with their insights in dealing with discrimination is to allow the Holy Spirit to relinquish prejudices that have been innate and permit the grace of the Gospel to cleanse our hearts from such demeaning mindsets. We are exhorted in 2 Corinthians 5:16, "Therefore, from now on we regard no one according to the flesh" (NKJV). We are also exhorted in Romans 12:3, "[t]o everyone who is among you not to think of himself more highly than he ought to think, but to think soberly as God has dealt to each one a measure of faith" (NKJV). As followers of Christ, this now becomes our new perspective toward those who differ from ourselves.

Eradicating Discrimination and Racism

The account of the Samaritan woman's conversation with Jesus in John chapter four has interesting dynamics that one can observe. In this record, we identify a common problem which all societies struggle with concerning discrimination touching the issues of worship, status, racism, and gender.

At first, as we read this account, we see how the Samaritan woman reacts to Jesus's request for a drink of water as she could see that he was Jewish. She reacted to his natural features, seeing that he was a Jew. This is a common problem in today's world. In the times which this account was recorded, we learn that Jews did not associate with the Samaritans for fear of being "contaminated." Her question directed at Jesus was valid, yet it appears to be racist. "How is it that You, being a Jew, ask a drink from me, a Samaritan woman? For Jews have no dealings with Samaritans" (John 4:9, NKJV).

As we read Jesus's response, we don't see him defending his skin color. We don't see him apologizing for being Jewish and for not being a Samaritan. He doesn't bother to make it an issue like this woman did. Instead, he see's past her reactional racist remarks. He perceives her real need—she wanted to be loved. He offers her what she really needed—a drink of living water that nothing of this world could give her.

As the conversation goes on, they discuss worship (religion). Again, Jesus does not put down the worship of her people but points to the new thing that God is about to do for all people. "Those who worship him, must worship him in spirit and truth" (John 4:24, NKJV). This implies that it would no longer be about a certain location in order to have the right site for worshipping God.

As we read further into this account, another concern is presented as shown when the disciples returned from their trip to the nearby town which touches gender issues as they "marveled that he talked with a woman" (John 4:27). Jesus did not even entertain their prejudice. His response to them was to help the disciples to focus on the souls of all people in their need for salvation.

Within this account, we see Jesus put to silence the issues of discrimination, be it racial, place of worship, or gender. Let's look again at his words, "Those who worship him, must worship him in spirit and truth" (Vs. 24, NKJV). Those who worship him are those who worship him in spirit and truth. What does that mean? Is this a special method? Who are "those" who worship him? Do we not see how this was the same principle from an earlier conversation that Jesus held with Nicodemus, "unless one is born again, he cannot see the kingdom of God" (John 3:3, NKJV)?

The issue at hand is that unless one is born again, it is impossible to worship God in spirit and truth. In spirit and truth means that we have been made the righteousness of God. For without this righteousness, no person has any ability or privilege to approach God.

Jesus points to the issue of the matter. This was not merely about being honest and sincere in our worship of God nor was it about being at the right location or born of a certain race or gender or having a certain status. We need the critical part—we must be born again and we must receive his righteousness in order to worship him in spirit and truth. This fundamental truth eradicates all discrimination and the assumption that sincerity is good enough. For all human beings are in the same position.

All people, no matter race or gender, are unable to worship God in spirit and truth if they are not born again. If we cannot understand that, then we are blinded by our own biases and ethnic systems of prejudiced attitudes toward those not like ourselves. God's heart is for all to be saved and restored through redemption in his blood. Dignity and equality then become restored to all who, having been born again, have received salvation through faith in his name.

Discrimination was a social problem in the times that Jesus walked on this earth, and as we know, it is still a problem in our generation. Ever since the event of the fall recorded in Genesis chapter three, this problem of discrimination has always existed. Rick Joyner shares the following:

> There are two foundations to racism. The first is pride in one of its most base forms—pride in the flesh. It is judging others by externals, which is the ultimate form of pride. It is basic form, pride is simply the statement that we feel sufficient within ourselves, that we do not really need God, or anyone else. This creates an obvious barrier between ourselves and others. The second foundation to racism is fear. Insecurity is a result of the Fall and the separation between God and man. The insecure are afraid of those who are different and those they cannot control. Racism is a powerful and deeply woven combination of both pride and fear. Trust is the bridge that makes relationship possible. You can have love and even genuine forgiveness, but if you do not have trust, a relationship is impossible. Fear and pride tear down the trust that makes relationships impossible, therefore creating division. The cross of Christ confronts and overcomes both the pride of man and his insecurity. The Holy Spirit was sent to the world to convict the world of sin, because it is the revelation of our sin that drives us to the cross to find grace and forgiveness. This destroys our pride by establishing our dependency on the Savior, which also restores our trust in him. The

deeper the cross works in us, the more humble and secure in His love we will become.[24]

The love of God is the only way we are able to become secure and whole persons. "There is no fear in love; but perfect love casts out fear" (1 John 4:18a, NKJV). Perfect love comes from God, for only he is perfect and has perfectly loved us. Through this kind of love, we are able to resolve issues of racism. God's love will always lead us to change, and his grace removes all ungodly attitudes we have toward those who are different than that of ourselves. Michael Cromwell presents the following on a biblical approach to racism:

> While the nation can help itself by being fair with its people, the individual is always encouraged to reach out to others—to not only be fair and just in dealing with one another but loving and compassionate as well. Instead of fighting racism with anger or reserve or outright protests one way to be proactive in the fight against racism, would be to be openly kind, compassionate, and considerate of the victims of racial oppression be they real or perceived. Wherever they are—at the workplace, or in the street—the real and perceived victims of racism should be treated kindly and fairly at all times. It is not a matter of respect, out of love for one's fellow man.[25]

We need to honestly look at ourselves and ask the Holy Spirit to search within our own hearts if we maintain any unrenewed mindsets

[24] Joyner, Rick, *Overcoming Racism* Copyright © 1996, E-book Edition 2010, Publisher: MorningStar Publications a Division of MorningStar Fellowship Church, Fort Mill, SC 29715 www.MoringStarMinistries.org, Part I—Racism and The Spirit of Death

[25] Cromwell, Michael, *A Biblical Approach to Racism.* Copyright © 1999, Publisher: Xlibris Corporation, www.Xlibris.com

of racism without pointing blame at others and saying, "Look! They are racist!" If we sincerely look in the mirror and allow the correction of the Holy Spirit to adjust our thinking toward certain people, our perspective will change for the better. Past experiences tend to build prejudice while we discriminate without realizing it. In dealing with racist mindset lurking within, David Platt states:

> Each person's value is grounded not in skin color or ethnic background but in the face that we are created in God's image. This unity is also evident in that every person, regardless of his or her God-given distinctions, is a descendant of the first man, Adam. Therefore, God commands us to love our neighbor, which includes doing the most loving thing—sharing the gospel. Our inherent equality as God's creatures and our common need of his saving grace means that we should repent of any sense of superiority we might feel toward others.[26]

In order for the church to maintain biblical equality, it must face discrimination in all areas with the truths of redemption. We are challenged to be rid of it, even to the core of any opinions or prejudices we have developed over the years within our own lives. Author E. Stanley Jones challenges believers in regard to a superiority complex as a hindrance to their own Christian witness:

> Service to man is light, but emphasis on service may so shut out fellowship with God and take its place that the light turns to darkness. The belief in the superiority of the Christian faith is light, but if that belief makes us have a superiority

[26] Platt, David. *A Compassionate Call to Counter Culture in a World of Racism.* Copyright © 2015, by David Platt. Publisher: Tyndale House of Publisher, Inc. www.tyndale.com

complex toward other races, then that light turns to darkness.[27]

All people have been a victim of racism or have held racist and prejudiced thinking in some form or another. We as a church need to seek the healing of brokenness from the effects of sin of which some of its symptoms are racism, prejudice, and discrimination. In his book, *The Reconstruction of the Church*, E. Stanley Jones states the following:

> The church at Antioch became redemptive because Paul became redemptive. A woman in Korea rapped on the door of a church and asked: 'Is this the place where they mend broken hearts?' The answer from within should be: 'Yes, we specialize in mending broken hearts, broken homes, broken relationships, broken bodies, and broken hopes. This is our chief business—all else is secondary.' The chief business of the church is redemption—the mending of broken everything.[28]

The church is meant to be a place of healing as individuals come into wholeness through understanding what redemption means in light of the new creation realities. When these truths begin to shape the heart, forgiveness becomes a natural response to those we have been offended by. We begin to realize that due to a lack of God's love, hurt people will hurt people. As this process of grace and

[27] Jones, Stanley E. *The Christ of the Mount—A Living Exposition of Jesus' Words as the Only Practical Way of Life.* Festival Edition Published 1981. Copyright ©1931. Copyright renewal 1958 by E. Stanley Jones. Publisher: Festival Books, Abingdon Nashville, pg. 241

[28] Jones, E. Stanley. *The Reconstruction of the Church—On What Pattern?* Copyright © 1970 by Abingdon Press. Publisher: Abingdon Press, Nashville TN pp. 100–101

healing goes on, with the cooperation of the Hol͟
cover the power to forgive what seems unforgiveable. ͟
Racism in the Church, Kenneth Copeland touches on the ͟
of forgiveness:

> When it comes to winning the war against the
> spirit of division, forgiveness is one the mightiest
> weapons in our spiritual arsenal. As believers, we
> need to be using it all the time.[29]

Harboring offense only hinders our spiritual progress to wholeness. In keeping with biblical unity, we can know that Christ desired for oneness among all believers based on the work of the cross and that this was made possible. The middle wall of partition has been removed. We are brought back into unity with one another. In her book, *The Unstoppable Church*, Marie Brown states:

> Jesus came and taught oneness. He prayed for
> oneness. Then Jesus went to the cross to make
> oneness possible. The work of the cross spiritu-
> ally restored us to a place of oneness with God
> and oneness with each other. It redeemed us back
> to God (washing away sin) and abolished the
> wall separating us from him… We must receive
> all the redemptive work of Christ—not just a
> part. Once we understand who we are (one with
> Christ), then we can start actively embracing by
> faith our oneness with others in the Body (1 Cor.
> 12:4–27) and experience the oneness in plurality
> for which Jesus died. The more real the work of

---

[29] Copeland, Kenneth. *Racism in the Church—Kill the Root, Destroy the Tree.* E-book Edition. Copyright © 2016 by Kenneth Copeland. Published in Partnership with: Harrison House Publishers, Tulsa, OK 74145 and Kenneth Copeland Publications, Fort Worth, TX 76192-0001, Chapter 8

...ss is to us, the more we realize that it is for ...r us together.[30]

The writer believes it is crucial for leaders of churches and Christian organizations to evaluate how the issues of discrimination are being handled among their own gatherings. As Christian leaders, we need to consider if we are even aware of it among our own circles. We cannot avoid it and hope it will go away. It is therefore crucial that we begin to put to practice the values of biblical equality. Instead of treating one another according to how we differ, we ought to treat each other with the dignity to which Christ has restored each one. We need to aspire to become the compassion of Christ, which opens our eyes to those among us who are seemingly ignored within our own churches and reach out to them as equals according to faith in Christ (see Appendix B).

As we identify with the new birth identity in Christ in ourselves and with other believers, regardless of race, status, or gender, a mutual and equal relationship forms based on faith in Christ alone. We do more than cooperate and coexist; we become one in Christ. Observing Jesus's prayer in the garden of Gethsemane:

> I do not pray for these alone, but also for those who will believe in Me through their word; that they all may be one, as You, Father are in Me, and I in you, that they also may be one in Us, that the world may believe that You sent Me. And the glory which You gave Me, I have given them, that may be one just as We are one. I in them, and You in Me; that they may be made perfect in one, and that the world may know that You have sent Me, and have loved them as You have love me. (John 17:20–23, NKJV)

---

[30] Brown, Marie. *The Unstoppable Church.* Copyright © 2010 by H. Marie Brown. Publisher: Marie Brown Ministries Inc., Columbia, SC. 29260, USA, pp. 29, 33

His prayer expressed his heart and will for those yet to come to faith in him and was that we would be one as he and the Father were one. This beautiful picture of the oneness of the Father and the Son and the Holy Spirit would be embodied in his believers all over the world, crossing all ethnic barriers which sin has created. Christ's love negates any prejudice and empowers us to exemplify and personify the unity of our faith in him. Our redeemed status, our citizenship in heaven, based upon our being born again brings us into a common ground with one another as his redeemed community.

4

In His Covenant

U p to this point, we have discussed biblical equality based on being born again as our newfound identity in Christ. That no matter our race, tribe, status, gender, or locale, as believers, we are equal in our position in Christ. Being in Christ is the emphasis. Considering these biblical truths, this author will highlight what is also crucial to our common faith in Christ—all believers are joined together in his covenant.

Every believer no matter their ethnicity, status, gender, or natural birthplace, is included in the New Covenant. Understanding our position in the New Covenant, we will see how unnecessary it is to assent a "spiritual jurisdiction view." In light of knowing who we are in Christ, we need to recognize the significance of the New Covenant to which God has brought us into through Christ. For this is the core of our oneness and equality, which we share with each other in Christ.

First of all, substantial to the study of biblical covenant, this truth is central: the old and new covenant are both God's covenant. These covenants were not initiated by mankind.

Secondly, both covenants are founded in the person of Who we are in covenant with—God in Christ.

The book of Hebrews brings profound light to the new covenant of which all believers in Christ are included. The writer of Hebrews gives a brief overview of the old covenant to explain its fulfilment in Christ and how a new covenant has been established through the blood of his sacrifice.

In Hebrews 8:6–13, we read that the first covenant was instituted for atonement and then a second covenant was established for our redemption. The first covenant had been made obsolete, being replaced by the second covenant—a new covenant. The second is a better covenant; it is based on better promises. However, both covenants were initiated by God himself.

We need to ask: Why did God do that? What was the reason for establishing a new covenant? What does this have to do with us? Before we answer these questions, we need to define what a covenant is.

Covenant defined: a formal agreement, contact, or promise in writing; theology, an agreement which brings about a relationship of commitment between God and his people. The Jewish faith is based on the biblical covenants made with Abraham, Moses, and David.

Phrases: Old Covenant—Christian Theology, the covenant between God and Israel in the Old Testament. New Covenant— Christian Theology, the covenant between God and the followers of Christ.[31]

We learn from this definition that covenant is, first of all, a formal agreement; in other words, it is a binding promise between two parties to do or not to do certain things specified. Historically, national covenants between nations have been made.

Today, we call them treaties or solemn pledges. Covenants are usually made for a legal and binding agreement of validity, especially under an official seal. In ancient times, a sacrifice of an animal or a token gift from one's personal resources in exchange was made to seal a covenant. Today, in much of the world, a ring is used to signify a marriage covenant, and a certificate is signed for the documented legal proof of that marital union.

---

[31] *Oxford Dictionary*. Copyright 1998, 2003, 2005, 2010. Oxford University Press, Great Clarendon Street, Oxford, pg. 401

The Oxford Dictionary, previously viewed, also clarified what covenant is meant biblically; that within Christian theology, the study of covenant has to do with a covenant between God and his people both in the Old and New Testaments. In the Bible, the term *covenant* is scattered throughout its pages from beginning to end. Covenant is a crucial element to our foundation of our faith in Christ. It is also a key component to our redeemed spiritual status and new Christlike identity as born-again believers. When we comprehend the covenant that God brought us into through Christ, we become confident in who we are in him as believers.

God is Faithful to Covenant

Before we continue to outline covenant as seen in the Bible, we need to turn our attention to the God of the covenant. Question: Do we realize that covenant was God's idea? We must understand that God is faithful to covenant. Our faithful God does not break his promises.

> For just as the rain and snow fall from heaven and do not return there without saturating the earth and making it germinate and sprout, and providing seed to sow and food to eat, so My word that come from My mouth will not return to Me empty, but it will accomplish what I please and will prosper in what I sent it to do. (Isaiah 55:10–11, NKJV)

God always keeps his Word. Titus 1:2 states, "God who cannot lie." Our God is a God of truth. He is truth.[32] Our God of truth is a covenant-keeping God. He is able to carry out his word. This is legitimized in the creation account. Genesis 1, he spoke, and it happened as he declared it so. He also blessed what he created. Our God blesses

---

[32] John 14:6

what he does. His blessing is on his Word and the fulfillment of his Word. He means what he says. His words are not empty, and they are not a waste of expression. As believers, we can have total confidence in our covenant-keeping God. The Israelites also had to learn this about God who delivered them out of Pharaoh's hand:

> Know therefore that the Lord your God is God, the faithful God who keeps covenant and stead-fast love with those who love him and keep his commandments, to a thousand generations (Deuteronomy 7:9, ESV)

This was a new concept for Israel to grasp about God, for they had been in bondage to Egypt for up to four hundred years. Although he had delivered them, they would still need to learn to trust him for their future and that he would not abandon them in the wilderness. They entered in a school of learning about the faithfulness of God, their Deliverer. *Expositor's Bible Commentary* gives the following:

> This covenantal Lord is "the God," i.e., the one and only God. Also, he is a God who is characterized by a fixed commitment to his promises. He is trustworthy and reliable. He demonstrates this dependability in the way he deals with his covenantal citizens.[33]

The Psalmist wrote of God's faithfulness to covenant:

> He remembers His covenant forever…He remembered His holy promise. (Psalm 108:8,42, NKJV)

He will ever be mindful of His covenant…

---

[33] *Expositor's Bible Commentary*. Deuteronomy 7:9 (13 vol. series). Copyright © 1998–2017. Olive Tree Bible Software

He sent redemption to His people; He has commanded His covenant forever… (Psalm 111:5b, 9, NKJV)

Forever, O Lord, Your word is settled in heaven. Your faithfulness endures to all generations… (Psalm 119:89,90a, NKJV)

We can rest assured that our God is able to fulfill his Word. We only need to trust him.

How Covenant Started in the Bible

In understanding that God truly means what he says, we start by reading in Genesis 2:17 where he warns Adam and Eve not to eat of the forbidden fruit of the tree of knowledge of good and evil. He warned that if they ate of its fruit, they would surely die. As we read along the creation account, we discover in chapter three that Adam and Eve failed the test of obedience as the serpent deceived them. They chose to listen to his lies and disobey God's Word. Although they did not physically die at once, death did come. Death came in a three-fold dynamic.

Spiritual death was the first dynamic where they became separated from their source of spiritual life. Eventually, their bodies would die, and consequently, their souls would be separated from their body into an eternal separation from God in the lake of fire. God gave the warning; they did not heed, death came. Subsequently, they also become subjects to the one who deceived them—Satan.

The first indication we have of the beginning of God's covenant is seen in Genesis chapter three. It began with a promise decreed by God himself. When Adam and Eve were on trial for their treason of disobedience to the God's Word, we find the first prophecy about the seed who would deliver them from Satan's bondage:

And I will put enmity between you and the woman, And between your seed and her Seed;

He shall bruise your head, And you shall bruise
His heel. (Genesis 3:15, NKJV).

God promised that he would raise up a seed who would crush
the head of Satan. This seed would be identified in scripture as the
promised deliverer—the Messiah—who would come and rescue
humanity from sin and Satan's rule over them.

In Genesis 3:24, we read that God made tunics of skin to clothe
the nakedness of Adam and Eve. This is the first significance of a
sealing of this covenant promise as it begins with the first sacrifice
that God had made. It took blood to seal that covenant. An innocent animal had to die in their place in order that they could be
covered, thereby providing atonement. For without this atonement,
they could not maintain their relationship with God.

God showed them what it would take to approach him due
their sin condition. Since they lost their righteousness, which gave
them this ability to stand in his presence, it would take the shedding
of the blood of a substitute sacrifice as this would enable them to
approach God. The promise of the deliverer to come was sealed by
the blood the lamb, the animal that God chose. Their sin condition
did not change; for now, they at least had atonement, and a sacrificial
system was set in place to remind them of God's covenant.

Notice: God chose it, not man. God made the promise, not
man. God ordained the covenant, not man. It is done in God's way,
not man's own inclination. We must understand that both religion
and cultural tradition is man's doing; it is not God's doing. The
only way that God will accept is his way and not man's independent
approach.

Moving on from there, the purpose of this covenant promise
decreed in Genesis 3:15 was about redeeming humanity from the
curse of sin and death. As time progressed in mankind's history, we
learn throughout the pages of the Bible how mankind began to drift
away from maintaining their relationship with God as they commenced doing their own thing. An example of this is seen in Genesis
chapters six through nine on the account of Noah building an ark by
God's command, because God sent a great flood upon the earth. One

can assume at this point in man's history that mankind obviously developed an ideology that "anything goes."

The Bible records how violent and wicked the earth had become. God judged the world with a destructive flood, sparing only Noah and his family—eight souls and a set of the various animals. We can accept that prior to this judgment, the people of Noah's time would not come to God his way—through the blood sacrifice as instituted since the time of the fall.

However, we see in scripture that God was specific about this kind of blood sacrifice, because it spoke of Christ who would come to be our final sacrifice. The first covenant merely covered our sins, but it did not remove our sins. It brought mankind a temporary covering, because the heart of mankind was utterly sinful. However, the Bible tells us "they did not continue in my covenant" (Hebrews 8:9), and in another place, "they went about to establish their own righteousness" (Romans 10:3b). Although the book of Hebrews speaks mainly of Israel, Romans 1:16–32 also reveals a broader view about the heart of mankind by their very own historical record. Since the beginning, mankind simply drifted away from the covenant of God.

However, God did not give up on humanity. In his faithfulness, God did not leave the human race to remain lost forever. In his plan of redemption, he focused his attention to one man to reestablish his covenant with. He had in mind to fulfill his original promise from Genesis 3:15 to raise up the seed. Instead of dealing with them as a whole society, he fixed his focus on one family through one man—Abram.

To summarize, we find in Genesis chapters twelve through fifteen how God called Abram out of his kindred and country. He told him to arise and walk the land that he will give to him. He promised Abram that he would become a father of many nations with his wife Sarai who was barren. At this point, he was about to reestablish his covenant which he made in the Garden of Eden through what seemed like an impossible situation. To help Abram have faith in his Word, he told him to look at the stars in the sky, including the sand on the seashore and, if possible, to try to count them. For his sake, in the night hours or in the heat of the day, when he felt doubtful of

God's Word, he would have something visual to always remind him of God's promise.

We must not forget as we look at Abram's life that God had one thing in mind—it was the redemption of the soul of mankind. Although they played a key role in God's plans and purposes, it wasn't only about Abram or his wife, Sarai. Remember, it was God (not Abram) who made this covenant.

Genesis 15:1–18, in summary, we find what God specified to Abram to prepare as a sacrifice and then caused him to fall into a deep sleep. This would be God's doing. Blood was shed, and the covenant was sealed.

We find in Genesis 17 how God changed their names from Abram to Abraham, from Sarai to Sarah. It was after this that they were able to conceive in their old age to bring forth a son who God would cause to prosper and bring forth the promised seed—the Deliverer/Messiah through this family line. We discover that within this chapter alone, thirteen times, God refers to this covenant as "My covenant"—another reminder that this is God's covenant. God also becomes more specific about his covenant, and his plan becomes clearer. Isaac is born, and the plan of redemption commences.

It would be years for Abraham to prove his trust in God in his Creator, his Covenant partner. We read in Genesis 22 how God asked Abraham to sacrifice his only son on an altar, the one who was chosen to be his heir of which would become the family line of the promised seed—the deliverer (Messiah). The establishment of this promise would require something from Abraham. It would be a costly requirement on Abraham's part. In biblical times and including many tribal people of today, a concept within covenant relationships is understood—what's yours is mine, what's mine is yours. This tenet is parallel to the account of God asking Abraham for his son Isaac:

> "Take your son," He said, "your only son Isaac, whom you love, go to the land of Moriah, and offer him there as a burnt offering on one of the mountains I will tell you about." (Genesis 22:2, HCSB)

God said to Abraham, "take your son…your only son." As we progress in this part of the story, we find Isaac asking where the sacrifice was. Abraham had such confidence in God that in his reply to Isaac, he says, "My son, God will provide himself a lamb" (vs. 8). However, it was not until Abraham actually bound his son and laid him on the altar, as he raised the knife to slay his son, an angel of the Lord stopped him from slaying Isaac. As the angel said to him:

> Do not lay your hand on the lad, or do anything
> to him, for now I know that you fear God and
> since you have not withheld your son, your only
> son from me (Gen. 22:12, NKJV).

We must understand that God was looking for trust. In covenant, there must be trust.

There must be proven faith. Abraham proved his faith and trust in God, his covenant partner. He feared God. It wasn't Abraham initiating this covenant with God, but rather, it was God making this covenant with Abraham. Abraham had to have understood that.

An exchange was made. The reason Isaac did not have to die was because he could not make atonement for his own sins with his own blood, because Isaac himself was not sinless. He needed a substitute sacrifice. Just as Abraham expected, God did provide them a sacrifice as we read how a ram, just a few yards from them, was found caught by the horns in a thicket. The ram was found to be without blemish. It was a male and was sacrificed instead of Isaac.

This significant event reveals a dynamic to this momentous test of Abraham's faith in God as it correlates with God's covenant with Abraham. Here, Abraham is acting on behalf of mankind. He is representing humanity to God. Remember God's promise in the Garden of Eden? We make the connection to the covenant concept—what's yours is mine, what's mine is yours—with God's statement to Abraham through the angel, "You have not withheld your son, your only son from me." Although Abraham did not sacrifice Isaac, what he did was symbolic enough to signify that nothing precious to him was withheld from God, because he feared God.

At the fold of this radical experience of his covenant relationship with God, Abraham names that location Jehovah-Jireh, meaning "The Lord will provide." This would be another reminder to Abraham and to the proceeding generations that God will provide. Provide what? There would come a day when the fulfillment of God's covenant to Abraham, including the rest of mankind, to send the deliverer. In this covenant deal, an exchange was required, the obligation on Abraham's part to not withhold his only son, the one in whose loins would bring forth the deliverer. From an eternal perspective, in light of redemption, the transaction was done.[34]

From this point, as we read in the books of Exodus, Leviticus, Numbers, and Deuteronomy of the Old Testament, we learn how God taught the children of Israel through Moses about the law of holiness regarding sacrificial law. It took blood to make atonement. God taught them what it would require to be able to come before his presence. This was in practice of maintaining their covenant relationship with him. If they wanted his blessing as his chosen ones, they were to be an example to the surrounding nations about coming to God his way; they were also to keep this covenant institution of the blood sacrifice. For generations, they also celebrated the annual Passover Meal as this was to remember the night of their deliverance from bondage to Pharaoh in Egypt.[35]

As we read the history books of the Old Testament, we discover that the children of Israel did not continue in this covenant as they continually walked away from God. They followed after the false gods of other nations. They were not faithful to God to walk in his ways. They did not want to be identified with God's covenant. Only when trouble came would it become a convenience to them. Eventually, as conditioned in the covenant,[36] their constant backsliding brought judgement and his blessing lifted. They were punished

---

[34] Kenyon, E. W. *What Happened from the Cross to the Throne.* Copyright 2010. Publisher: Kenyon's Gospel Publishing Society, Lynnwood WA. 98046-0973, www.kenyons.org, pp. 25–29

[35] Exodus 12

[36] Deuteronomy 28

for not keeping their part of their agreement with God, resulting in captivity to their enemies.

This now brings us to understand in the letter of the book of Hebrews of the New Testament why it has been stated in chapter eight that a new covenant made the old obsolete (Hebrews 8:13). Why? The children of Israel had a common issue as all other nations of the world; it was called a sin condition. They really could not please God as they agreed. It was time for things to change. Therefore, Hebrews teaches that the old covenant was a type of the new covenant. It was to lead us to Christ since it foreshadowed his priesthood through his fulfillment of the law, became the Final Sacrifice, and established by his blood this new covenant.[37]

New Covenant Established and Sealed

Mankind had proven they could not keep covenant with God simply because of their spiritual condition, that of the sinful nature. This condition along with their own choice to continue to sin reveals the need for a radical intervention. As Hebrews reveals:

> I will make a new covenant with the house of Israel and with the house of Judah—not according to the covenant I made with their fathers in the day when I took them by the hand to lead them out of the land of Egypt; because they did not continue in my covenant and I disregarded them. (Hebrew 8:8b–9, NKJV).

God had in mind from the beginning to redeem the human race from the curse of sin and death. He always had in mind to bring forth the promised deliverer as revealed through the numerous prophets' foretelling of the Messiah. History had proven that mankind is unable to change their sin condition. They also needed to realize

---

[37] Hebrews 7:11–28, 8:1–13, 10:1–10

their need for deliverance from sin, that they needed more than physical and political freedom. They needed more than a religious system of traditions and rituals. A spiritual freedom was needed that could only be attained through what God provided in the Messiah.

An outward ceremony could not remedy their sinful condition. Something deeper was needed.[38] Something that the blood of bulls and goats could not do was needed:

> Therefore, when He came into the world He said: sacrifice and offering You did not desire, but a body you have prepared for me (Hebrews 10:5, NKJV);

> For God so loved the world that He gave his only Son… (John 3:16a, NKJV).

This leads us into Luke's record of the last supper, also called the Lord's supper, as Jesus celebrated the Passover with his disciples in Luke 22:14–20. First, Jesus expressed the heart of God in his statement, "With desire I have desired to eat this Passover with you before I suffer" (vs. 15a, NKJV). The time of fulfillment had come to pass. The promised deliverer had come.

However, he says "this Passover." Why this one? Why was this Passover so special? Israel had celebrated previous Passovers for centuries. Why was this one different from the others?

Many speak of this account as the last supper; as true as that is, do we understand that this may also be the first supper? Perhaps this is why we call it the Lord's supper; after all, it is his covenant. Remember how it was God who caused Abraham to fall into a deep sleep while that first covenant was being established, that it was God who made that covenant? Therefore, with this Passover meal recorded in Luke 22, we see that it is the Lord who also established

---

[38] Kenyon, E. W. *What Happened from the Cross to the Throne.* Copyright 2010. Publisher: Kenyon's Gospel Publishing Society, Lynnwood, WA. 98046-0973, www.kenyons.org, pp: 49–57

the new covenant. A new covenant commenced. He anticipated this day. He delighted to do his Father's will. He had the bigger picture in mind. His sacrifice would institute this new covenant as it would be established in the blood of Christ.

He teaches his disciples the new way—the bread and the cup of remembrance. This would become a new kind of remembrance. No longer would it be about the Passover when God delivered Israel from Egypt, but it would be about the sacrifice of Jesus who became our Passover Lamb. It would be about our spiritual deliverance from bondage to sin and death.

"This is my body which was given for you" (vs. 19b, NKJV). Jesus was utterly sinless. He met the requirements as the final sacrifice for all mankind as our substitute. He would die in our place, "[a] body you have prepared for me" (Hebrews 10:5, NKJV). His body was prepared, and the time had come for this sacrifice to be made. "God will provide for Himself a lamb… In the Mount of the Lord it shall be provided" (Genesis 22:8,14, NKJV). Jesus was crucified on Mount Calvary. It would be God offering his Son on our behalf. Love in action. Love would sacrifice himself for our eternal spiritual redemption.

"This cup is the new covenant in my blood which is shed for you" (vs. 20, NKJV). Jesus's blood was shed to seal the new covenant. It was shed for us not only for our atonement where we receive mere forgiveness. "The Deliverer will come out of Zion and He will turn away ungodliness from Jacob; for this My covenant with them when I take away their sins" (Romans 11:26–27, NKJV). The key element in the new covenant is that we become more than forgiven; even greater, our sins have been taken away. Not only have we been forgiven, have had our sins removed, but we are redeemed eternally and are made a new creation.

"If any man be in Christ, He is a new creation. Old things are passed away, behold all things have been made new" (2 Corinthians 5:17, NKJV). The sin condition is no longer an issue. A new reality of our spiritual condition in our redemption has been implemented. "This is the covenant, I will make with them after those days, says the Lord: I will put my laws into their hearts and in their mind's I will

THE BIRTH THAT COUNTS

write them and then He adds, their sins and their lawless deeds I will remember no more" (Hebrews 10:16, NKJV). This is speaking of the new creation reality within the new covenant.

To be in Christ means that we are in the new covenant. When we believe the Gospel, repent of our sins, and accept Christ as our personal Lord and Savior, we become born again and are made a new creation. Consequently, we are brought into covenant with God through Christ:

> [y]ou were without Christ, being aliens from the commonwealth of Israel and strangers from the covenants of promise, having no hope and without God in the world. But now in Christ Jesus, you who once were far off have been brought near by the blood of Christ. (Ephesians 2:12–13, NKJV).

All Nations Now Included

Another key element about the new covenant is that all nations are accepted through their faith in Christ. It is a sobering fact that the old covenant involved only one group of people, namely the Jews. All other nations of the world, termed by the Jewish nation as Gentiles, were not in covenant with God as Paul notes that we (who are not Jews) were "strangers from the covenants of promise" (Ephesians 2:12, NKJV). All Gentile nations were not a part of the covenant arrangement that God instituted with Israel. He chose one nation to be set apart for himself to be in covenant with him. They were to be his example to the world about living according to the standards of holiness that God revealed to them. They utterly failed God. They were unable to change their hearts. They were no more different in their lack of righteousness than those of the Gentiles. They continually breached their covenant with God.

The Old Testament sacrificial system provided them a temporary covering, yet it never changed their sinful condition. They needed to realize that they needed something deeper. For Israel, instead of crying out for this change, most of them gave in to that sinful nature and went their own way. Therefore, Romans says, "What then? Are we better than they? Not at all. For we have previously charged both Jews and Greeks that they are all under sin" (3:9, NKJV). And in another place, "For God has committed them all to disobedience, that He might have mercy on all" (11:32, NKJV).

As we recall the discussion Jesus held with Nicodemus about the importance of being born again, we can understand that God views the human race in one of two categories:

1.   We are either born again—In Christ's covenant and made righteous by faith in his blood sacrifice, "the righteousness of God, through faith in Jesus Christ, to all and on all who believe, for there is no difference" (Roman 3:22, NKJV)

Or,

2.   We are still dead in our sins, "For all have sinned and fallen short of the glory of God" (Romans 3:23, NKJV).

There is no middle ground. In God's eyes, there is no difference. There is not one nation or certain personalities favored over another, "For there is no partiality with God" (Romans 2:11, NKJV). All are required to believe and receive Jesus as Lord and Savior if they want to be accepted into his kingdom and yet for those who have received him are joined with him in the new covenant.

It is crucial that we understand what it means to be in his covenant. Spiritually speaking, the only "spiritual jurisdiction" that the Gentiles were under was the kingdom of darkness. Now, because of Christ's substitutionary work, we are no longer under the dominion of Satan which includes this world. Being in his covenant causes all believers to become set apart into the kingdom of God—a new kind of spiritual jurisdiction that we identify with as Jesus said, "My kingdom is not of this world. If my kingdom were of this world, My servants would fight...but now My kingdom is not from here" (John 18:36, NKJV).

We now must learn what it means to be a child of God in this new covenant. How we defined ourselves prior to accepting Christ as Lord and Savior now changes in perspective of being born again—a new creation (see 2 Corinthians 5:17). Therefore, this now affects how we view other believers in Christ who are not from our birthplace or of our race, tribe, status, gender, or age. Instead of being limited by a "spiritual jurisdiction view," we are liberated in the new creation realities within the new covenant, that those believers in Christ who are different from us are also in the same covenant with God. We hold the same covenant privileges. Kelley Varner also writes:

> Finally, in Christ there is neither Jew nor Greek; but there is still Jew, and there is still Greek (gentile), and we are different! I am not a Jew by nationality or race, and thus I cannot fully feel the heart of my brother who is. Most of us "Greeks" are woefully ignorant of the rich legacy of Jewish history. Let us value Jewish culture, custom and ethnicity. Let us appreciate and learn more about our mutual spiritual heritage in the Old Testament Scriptures. As we do, let us maintain that the most powerful commonality between Jew and Greek is based upon the saving blood of the Messiah Jesus Christ. God has not called either group to renounce their nationalities or basic cultural preferences, but to focus upon the cross of Christ, that cause of the kingdom, and the love for each other that Jesus promised would be the identifying feature of his true disciples (Jn. 13:35)[39]

1 John 1:7 teaches us, "If we walk in the light as he is in the light; we have fellowship with one another; and the blood of Jesus

---

[39] Varner, Kelley. *The Three Prejudices.* Copyright © 1997. Destiny Image Publishers, Inc. Shippensburg, PA. 1997 pg. 160

Christ his Son cleanses us from all sin" (NKJV). This is the fundamental nature of the new covenant which we have in Christ with one another—we have fellowship. The word *fellowship* in the original Greek, *Koinania,* means partnership.[40] We must understand that without the shed blood of Christ, we continue to remain lost and remain dead in our sin under Satan's domain. Our biological factors could not change our depraved spiritual condition for us. However, Jesus's blood changed this for us in that we who have accepted his substitutionary work are delivered from that dominion of darkness. Subsequently, we are brought into a oneness with each other in that we are each born again, and together, we are brought into the new covenant of his grace. Though this, we have equal privilege and have partnership with one another in the new covenant.

If we embrace this substantial element of our fellowship with one another in Christ, our perspective changes, knowing that our partnership is not conditional to being a "gatekeeper," including the origin of our birthplace, race, tribe, status, or gender. Instead, our partnership corresponds to the nature of our spiritual birth as we share the mutuality of our being one in Christ in his covenant. It is the blood of Christ which redeems and brings all believers into the new covenant. *Expositors Bible Commentary* states:

> The Greek word koinōnia ("fellowship") is used again, suggesting that two parties "have something in common" (Marshall, 105)[41]

Our commonality and oneness are within the reality of being brought into the new covenant through being born again by faith in Christ. We begin to grasp the Father's heart that his desire is for all nations to be redeemed from the tyranny of Satan and sin, and

---

[40] Strong's word number: g2842 "koinonia" from g2844 "partnership": *Olive Tree Enhanced Strong's Dictionary.* Copyright © 1998–2017. Olive Tree Bible Software

[41] *Expositor's Bible Commentary.* 1 John 1:6–7, (13 vol. series). Copyright © 1998–2017. Olive Tree Bible Software

THE BIRTH THAT COUNTS

consequently, we are restored to his kingdom. It is his heart that all inequality, discrimination, and dividing factors of all forms among humanity be eradicated with his healing grace and love as Christ is received in our hearts. Paul exhorts:

> [t]o everyone who is among you, not to think of himself more highly than he ought to think... so we, being many, are one body in Christ, and individually members of one another. (Romans 12:3a,5, NKJV)

> For as the body is one and has many members, but all members of that one body, being many, are one body, so also is Christ. For by one Spirit, we were all baptized into one body—whether Jews or Greeks, whether slaves or free—we have all been made to drink into one Spirit. (1 Corinthians 12:12–13, NKJV).

Paul speaks to both the Roman and Corinthian believers of the necessity to recognize the many members of the Body of Christ, how each member has been brought together by the same Spirit. As individual members, we share a oneness with all believers in Christ as citizens of the kingdom of God within his covenant—therein is equality.

E. Stanley Jones writes:

> By the surrender of cultural differences—barbarian or Scythian. The Scythian was cultured and the barbarian was not, so this created a cleavage. But in the new order, the kingdom, there is no room for that cultural division.[42]

---

[42] Jones, E. Stanley. *The Unshakeable Kingdom*. Copyright 1972 by Abingdon Press. Publisher: McNett Press, Bellingham, WA. 98277, pg. 85

All believers in Christ are brought into this covenant, which annihilates any division. We are in covenant with another by the Spirit of Christ who redeemed us through his blood. Malcom Smith writes:

> The new covenant describes a union between God and man so complete as to be paralleled to the glory of God dwelling in the tabernacle and the temple of the old covenant. The bodies of men and women have become the dwelling place of the Holy Spirit... A man or woman could not imagine such a privilege under the old covenant; the glory of God lived in a tent and later a house that they went to; to say that the glory was within them would be beyond comprehension. In all that we do, in all our relationships, we are the bearers of the divine presence. We must never think of ourselves apart from our absolute unity with the Spirit of Christ.[43]

How beneficial it becomes when we are conscious that each of us carries within us his divine presence. By this, we are kept in unity with one another through the covenant of which we are brought into by the blood of Christ. Being in his covenant also means that we are all birthed spiritually into his family. We no longer related with one another according to the flesh but according to the redemption we obtain in Christ. Our conduct toward one another is that we are of the household of God (see Appendix C).

Knowing the significance of every believer's role in the new covenant through the blood of Christ, we ascertain that individuals are not to be preferred due their biological distinctions.

Individuals are not given entitlement as "gatekeepers" in the kingdom of heaven for their gender, status, tribe or race, or any-

---

[43] Smith, Malcom, *The Lost Secret of the New Covenant.* Copyright 2002. Publisher: Harrison House, Inc. Tulsa, Oklahoma, 74153, pg. 197

thing which has been esteemed by the world's standards and endorsement. The "spiritual jurisdiction view" is no longer a question when we know our true spiritual position in Christ "and raised us up together and made us sit together in the heavenly places in Christ Jesus" (Ephesians 2:6, NKJV). "Together" is the emphasis which the author makes. There is no separation or marginalization of any person according to the redemption we are brought into in the new covenant through the blood of Christ.

If we truly believed that God shows no partiality, can we not do the same? Partiality (discrimination in any form) is not uniform to God's character. Nor does this approach express his heart for all people. He created all equal. When we as people lift up one race over another, are we not being partial or racist? Perhaps discriminative? When we entitle that one race is legitimized additional rights and privileges to minister the things of God because of their race, are we not limiting others whom he also chooses?

When we are partial, we subtlety exclude others; consequently, we become out of sync with the essence of the new covenant. Partiality only breeds contempt and does not express the heart of the new covenant realities for all believers. Reversal of superiority complex attitudes will bring individuals on a level of equal opportunity by embracing new creation truths realized in our common redeemed status in Christ.

In light of the new covenant, as believers in Christ, we need not to consent to the ideology that one has "extra rank" in matters of spiritual authority because of their physical national heritage. However, whenever when we as believers choose to believe, resting our faith in the finished work of Christ, we corporately walk in that divine spiritual authority. It is from that place that the limits of racial and social discriminations cease. There is no need to distinguish one over another. Instead, we as individuals can bless and encourage one another in our common faith in Christ. We begin to understand that we equally benefit all that is rightfully ours in his covenant. Being in his covenant attributes all believers equal privilege and equal opportunity.

5

Our Privilege in Prayer—
The Prayer of the Righteous

We have discussed that being born again through faith in Christ results in being included in the new covenant. We have also reviewed that all believers in Christ are made citizens of heaven, thereby making us equal in Christ, allotting all believers a oneness within that redeemed community. When understood, these certainties which begin to materialize among the family of God produces outcomes of biblical equality, Christian unity, and equal opportunity.

Having the status of being heavenly citizens enables all of God's people to walk in their spiritual authority in the name of Jesus. The "spiritual jurisdiction view" claims that spiritual authority can only be activated by the permission of a "gatekeeper," the individual who is native to the region they are from. We will now observe true biblical spiritual authority and see how a believer is not limited in operating in divine spiritual authority based upon a person's native relations to a region.

Although the scriptures teach us that we have spiritual authority in his name, we need to unfold the realities of what this truly means. What is authority? What does this spiritual authority entail? How is this realized in the prayer life of the believer in Christ?

Original Authority

Before we begin this session, it is essential to review original authority. People have been misguided in knowing what true spiritual authority in God's kingdom means. Therefore, it is necessary to examine authority as this has been part of the problem to which the author seeks to address and examine by definition and in view of the scriptures.

The Oxford Dictionary defines authority as the power or right to give orders, make decisions, and enforce obedience; the right to act in a specified way, delegated from one person or organization to another; official permission; sanction.[44]

This definition speaks of authority within the natural systems of this world. As long as we live on this earth, we will always be subject to delegated authority, and in some measure, we will also be entrusted with similar types of authorized responsibility. Official and governmental authority as shown in scripture is orchestrated by God, and we are instructed to obey these civil authorities.[45]

The intent of this book is not to nullify these types of authorities that are set in place that are meant to ensure that structural order in society. Watchman Nee gives this insight regarding earthly authority:

> The symbols for subjection to earthly authorities are fourfold: taxes to whom taxes are due, revenue to whom revenue is due, respect to whom respect is due, and honor to whom honor is due. A Christian obeys the law not only to avoid God's wrath but also for the sake of conscience. his conscience reproves him if he is disobedient. Hence, we must learn to be subject to local authorities. The children of God should not care-

---

[44] *Oxford Dictionary*. Copyright © 1998, 2003, 2005, 2010. Oxford University Press, Great Clarendon Street, Oxford, pg. 107
[45] Romans 13:1–7

lessly criticize or denounce the government. Even the police on the streets are instituted by God for they are commissioned to a specific task. When the tax-collectors or revenue inspectors come to us, what is our attitude toward them? Do we hear them as God's delegated authorities? Are we in subjection to them?[46]

Although, as believers, we are a part of the spiritual kingdom of heaven due to our spiritual new birth in Christ, we are not exempt from obeying civil authorities of this earth. Today, there is much that is changing within the laws of our western nations. As followers of Christ, the morals of God's Word and fundamentals of our faith in Christ cannot be compromised. When pressured by laws that contradict our conscience in God's Word, this is where we choose the spiritual laws of the kingdom of God to which we govern our lives.

What the author seeks to bring to light is that which pertains to matters of Christian ministry in relation to our spiritual authority in the kingdom of God as we will observe this in the scriptures. We will see how this applies in our lives as we follow Christ and continue his ministry to those unconverted who are not yet a part of his kingdom.

Two-fold biblical definitions of spiritual authority are revealed in Scripture.

First definition of spiritual authority:

> I have given you the authority to trample on serpents and scorpions and over all the power of the enemy and nothing shall by any means hurt you. (Luke 10:19, NKJV)

> And Jesus came and spoke to them saying, 'All authority has been given to Me in heaven and earth. (Matthew 28:18, NKJV)

---

[46] Nee, Watchman. *Spiritual Authority*. Electronic Edition. Copyright © 2014. Publisher: Christian Fellowship Publisher, Inc. New York, NY, Chapter 7

Authority derived from *Strong's* located in Luke 10:19 and Matthew 28:18: (in the sense of ability); privilege, i.e. (subjectively) force, capacity, competency, freedom, or (objectively) mastery (concretely, magistrate, superhuman, potentate, token of control), delegated influence.[47]

First of all, Matthew 28:18 speaks of the kind of spiritual authority which we are addressing has been given to Christ; "All authority has been given to me." It is crucial that we understand who holds this authority and to what extent. He holds all of it both in heaven and on earth.

The pronounced words of Jesus communicate that no person or being can claim to hold an allocated authority based on their origin of birth. Only Christ has that right as we recognize his proclamation—it has been given to him. It has also been given to him not only in heaven but also on earth.

We see in Luke 10:19 that we as believers in him are privileged as his followers to use the authority in his name which he has administered to us. Therefore, according to this definition indicated above from *Strong's* presents that the spiritual authority is delegated for the purpose of empowering those followers of Christ to carry out his mission. This is the privilege of all believers in Christ to operate in the power invested in Jesus's name with force, capacity, competency, and freedom. This power is not sourced within ourselves apart from him. Rather, it is given to us as his followers to simply continue the mandate of Christ. His ministry is continued through his people as we represent him on this earth. We are authorized to continue his work.

Second definition of spiritual authority:

> Now when he came into the temple, the chief priest and elders of the people confronted him as He was teaching and said, "By what authority are You doing these things? And who gave you this

---

[47] Strong's number g1849: ἐξουσία exousia; from 1832: *Olive Tree Enhanced Strong's Dictionary.* Copyright © 1998–2017. Olive Tree Bible Software

authority?" But Jesus answered and said to them, "I also will ask you one thing, which if you tell Me, I likewise will tell you by what authority I do these things; The baptism of John—where was it from? From heaven of from men?" (Matthew 21:23–24, NKJV)

Then they came again to Jerusalem. And as He was walking in the temple, the chief priest, the scribes and the elders came to him. And they said to him, 'By what authority are You doing these things? And who gave you this authority to do these things?' But Jesus answered and said to them, 'I will also ask you one question; then answer Me, and I will tell you by what authority I do these things. The baptism of John—was it from heaven or from men? Answer Me.' (Mark 11:27–29, NKJV)

Authority derived from Thayer's Greek–English Lexicon of the New Testament located in Matthew 21:23–24 and Mark 11:28–29—power: The power of authority (influence) and of right.[48]

Consider the dynamics surrounding these scriptural references in regard to Jesus's authority as it was called into question by the chief priests, scribes, and elders. Their questioning reveals to us the very heart of the matter. This relates to the same attitude we are confronted with in today's trendy "spiritual jurisdiction view." These men of leadership who questioned Jesus simply did not want to recognize Jesus's authority. However, what we learn from Thayer's definition above about the kind of authority which Jesus walked in, it had influence as he utilized his right to do the works of his Father in obedience to him.

---

[48] Thayer, H. Joseph. *Thayer's Greek-English Lexicon of the New Testament by Joseph Thayer.* Publisher: Hendrickson Publishers, Inc. Peabody, Massachusetts, #1849 "exousia": pg. 225

This influence and active power intimidated these learned men, for they had no legitimate spiritual authority in themselves.[49] They assumed the right and power of authority within the title and role which they held at the Jewish temple and the synagogues. Jesus made his point clear that he was authorized by his heavenly Father, and yet they would not believe him for their own envious hearts toward him. The reason Jesus could do the works of miracles was due to his simple obedience to his heavenly Father. This enabled him to operate in the force, capacity, competency, and freedom given to him by his heavenly Father. His authorization did not come from a person but from God who sent him.

The Origin of Divine Authority

First of all, as we read the Creation account in Genesis chapters one and two, we see our Creator creating the world by the word of his power. When the earth was ready, he then formed man. Immediately, Adam and Eve were given dominion—authority—to tend to the home which he prepared for them, "Let them have dominion" (Genesis 1:26). Through this account, we learn that authority originates from God, our Creator. Dr. LaDonna Osborn and Charles Capps share the following on this divine authority as given by God, our Creator:

> God instructed both Adam and Eve to subdue the earth and to have dominion over his creation. Inherent in this command is the reality that both men and women are endowed with God-given authority to rule and to have authority.[50]

---

[49] Johnson, David and VanVonderen, Jeff. *The Subtle Power of Spiritual Abuse.* Copyright 991. E-book Edition 2011. Publisher: Bethany House Publishers, 11400 Hampshire Ave South, Bloomington, Minnesota 55438, www.bethany-house.com, chapter 9

[50] Osborn, LaDonna C. *God's Big Picture.* Copyright © 2001 by LaDonna C. Osborn. Publisher: Osborn Publishers, Tulsa, OK. 74102, pg. 49

God created man to be god over the earth. Man wasn't put here as a worm in the dust. God created the earth and gave it to him. It became mans' to do with as he would, but God gave him some guidelines with the ability to carry them out...

God created man after his likeness, an exact duplication in kind. Then, what kind is God? Jesus said, God is a Spirit. You aren't God. You aren't equal with God in his divine attributes, but you are a spirit being under authority. You are able to partake of God's divine nature: righteousness.

Adam was subordinate to God. God created him, gave him all this authority and power, and said to him, 'Be god over the earth as I am God over the heavens.'[51]

What happened to this authority?

Genesis chapter three records the disobedience of Adam and Eve as they were deceived by Satan who came into their garden through the embodiment of a serpent. This treason brought them into subjection to Satan's rule, thereby losing their authority—ability to have dominion—which God had given to them originally. E. W. Kenyon gives the following explanation on the loss of man's dominion on earth:

The sin of Adam was the crime of High Treason. God had conferred upon him the authority to rule the universe. This Universe-wide dominion was the most sacred heritage God could give to man. Genesis 1:28 and Psalm 8:6. Adam turned

[51] Capps, Charles. *Your Spiritual Authority: Learn to Use Your God-given Rights to Live in Victory*. Copyright © 1980, 1982 by Charles Capps. Revised Copyright 1994. Publisher: Capps Publishing, England AK 72046, E-book Edition: Chapter 2

this legal dominion over into the hands of God's enemy, Satan...

Adam's sin of High Treason brought the entrance of Spiritual Death into the life of humanity...

Spiritual Death became universal. All humanity was identified with Adam in his Spiritual Death. Adam, the parent of man, the head of God's creation, had died spiritually. He had failed in his responsibility as the custodian of God's joy. Man, to whom he will give birth will possess the same nature...

Hebrews 2:14 speaks of Satan's holding the authority, the dominion of the realm of Spiritual Death.[52]

Kenneth E. Hagin also gives the following insight to this catastrophic moment:

In the beginning, Adam had the dominion over this world, and in that sense, Adam was made the 'god' of this world. But when Adam and Eve ate of the forbidden fruit, their eyes were opened and they knew good and evil (Gen. 3:6-7). God had told Adam and Even that in the day they ate of the fruit, they would die. Adam and Eve didn't die physically; they died spiritually. When they died spiritually, they were cut off or separated from God. By the act of disobedience, Adam forfeited his dominion on this earth to the devil. The Bible substantiates the fact that Adam sold out his dominion to Satan through disobedience

---

[52] Kenyon, E. W. *The Bible in the Light of Our Redemption.* Twenty-Eighth Printing. Copyright 2011 by Kenyon's Gospel Publishing Society. Printed in USA, pp. 26–30

and allowed Satan to become the god of this world.[53]

It is due to this tragic event in mankind's history that Satan is now the god of this world (2 Cor. 4:4). As he tempted Jesus, Satan speaks a fact about this gained title deed which he legally held:

> Then the devil, taking him up on a high mountain, showed him all the kingdoms of the world in a moment of time. All this authority I will give You and their glory; for this has been delivered to me. Therefore, if You will worship before me all will be Yours, (Luke 4:5–7, NKJV).

"It has been delivered unto me", this statement is in correlation to the high treason of Adam of that which was delivered to Satan the title of dominion in becoming god of this world. In another place, Jesus said to those fellow Jews who argued with him: "Ye are of your father the devil and the desires of your father you want to do."

> He was a murderer from the beginning and does not stand in the truth, because there is no truth in him. When he speaks a lie, he speaks from his own resources, for he a is a liar and the father of it. (John 8:44, NKJV)

This answers the question to what happened to the original authority to which man was delegated to have dominion with in the Garden of Eden. Ever since the loss of this dominion to Satan, there has been turmoil, pain, suffering, death, disease, deception, separation, evil of all sorts as this has all been a part of the curse unleashed on the earth. The most severe consequence of all was that mankind

---

[53] Hagin, Kenneth E. *The Triumphant Church.* Copyright 1993 Rhema Bible Church. Electronic Edition Published 2010, a.k.a. Kenneth Hagin Ministries Inc., Chapter 1

became separated from God and became a slave to Satan, having no way out from under his domain except through the remedy of Jesus's sacrifice. T. L. Osborn explains the following:

> Out in the un-believing world, Satan has author-
> ity to manipulate the un-converted. Why?
> Because they are his subjects. The original sin of
> Adam and Eve gave him lordship and suprem-
> acy over every person who does not embrace the
> redemptive work of Christ.[54]

Since we conclude that the world is under the sway of the wicked one,[55] we must realize that it is an error to believe that one has more spiritual authority in their native land than other believers who are not from there. David Johnson and Jeff VanVonderen, coauthors of *The Subtle Power of Spiritual Abuse*, give a balanced perspective as to how spiritual authority is seen in the life of a believer:

> The reason any of us is given spiritual authority
> is because God has led us through real-life experi-
> ences, by which He has revealed Himself and his
> living Word to be true. Spiritual authority is seen
> in the man or woman who says, by his or her life,
> 'God and his Word are true—I've proven them
> in the fibers of my being. I know there is hope
> in God!'[56]

---

[54] Osborn, T. L. *The Message That Works*. Copyright © 2004 by LaDonna C. Osborn. Publisher: Osborn Publishers, Tulsa, OK. 74102, pg. 309

[55] 1 John 5:19

[56] Johnson, David and VanVonderen, Jeff. *The Subtle Power of Spiritual Abuse*. Copyright 1991. E-book Edition 2011. Publisher: Bethany House Publishers, 11400 Hampshire Ave South, Bloomington, Minnesota 55438, www.bethany-house.com, Chapter 5

It is only as an individual who believes the Gospel they will come out from Satan's dominion and are conveyed into the kingdom of God as we read in Colossians:

> He has delivered us from the power of darkness and conveyed us into the kingdom of the Son of his love, in whom we have redemption through his blood, the forgiveness of sins (Colossians 1:13–14, NKJV).

We cannot exercise spiritual authority over lands and over individuals that choose not to believe the Gospel as Paul states:

> But even if our gospel is veiled, it is veiled only to those who are perishing, among whom the god of this age has blinded the minds of those who do not believe so they would not see the light of the glorious gospel of Christ, who is the image of God." (2 Corinthians 4:3–4, NET).

The reason they are spiritually blinded is because they chose not to believe. We cannot choose for them. God has given every individual the right to choose to believe the Gospel for themselves. However, when any person chooses to believe as they hear the Gospel, they will no longer be spiritually blinded in their minds by the god of this age, and they become free from Satan's dominion. Kenneth E. Hagin wrote:

> Some people today are getting into a ditch with some of the things they are doing in the name of spiritual warfare. Spiritual warfare is biblical. But some marvelous and dear Christians have gotten into excess by some extreme practices that are not biblical. Although a lot of these extremes are listed under what they call 'pulling down strongholds', they do not line up with what we read in the New

Testament. Some of these dear, misguided people believe they are actually pulling down entire strongholds over cities and nations through such excess in prayer as 'warring' tongues. Actually, we have no direct scriptural support for pulling down demonic strongholds over entire cities and nations, especially in the sense of warring tongues and yelling at the devil.[57]

Putting it into perspective, we understand from scripture that without our redemption through the blood of Jesus, we have no authority over the devil. However, it is due to this redemption that we are delivered from the powers of darkness and sin that we begin to simply walk in our authority in Christ. Spiritual authority stems from our being born again through faith in Christ. There is no need to acclaim "original spiritual authority" as a "gatekeeper." Neither is it necessary to include a carrying out of "extra actions" to assert this victory; we only need to rest in Christ's work. The Bible also does not teach us to exercise spiritual authority by attempting to bring down demonic realms over lands based on our own natural citizenship. No such person can acclaim having spiritual authority over regions due to the spiritual law that the whole human race is subject to Satan. Only until an individual hears and believes the Gospel repents of their sin and accepts Jesus as their Lord and Savior is when that individual comes out from the spiritual realm of Satan's domain.

Satan is defeated—spiritual authority regained through Christ. It is imperative to know that when applying spiritual authority, Satan is a defeated foe. We are not trying to gain a victory over him that Christ already accomplished. As believers, we simply assert that victory over darkness in the position which we already hold in Christ:

The reason the Son of God was made manifest (visible) was to undo (destroy, loosen, and dis-

---

[57] Hagin, Kenneth E. *The Triumphant Church*. Copyright 1993. Rhema Bible Church. Electronic Edition Published 2010, a.k.a. Kenneth Hagin Ministries Inc., Chapter 9

solve) the works the devil [has done]. (1 John
3:8, AMP)

What took place at Christ's death on the cross was more than a
paid ransom for our salvation. Included in his work was also a total
rendering of Satan's authority over our lives. The shout which Jesus
gave in his last moment on the cross at Calvary—"It is finished!"
(John 19:30)—was not an expression of exhaustion. This was a victorious shout which came from the depths of his being, declaring
over all eternity that the ransom for the human race was paid in full.
Satan's works had been made null and void.

> And having disarmed the powers and authorities,
> he made a public spectacle of them, triumphing
> over them by the cross. (Colossians 2:15, NIV).

Disarm from the Oxford Dictionary: take a weapon or weapons
away from (a person, force or country).[58]

This word, *disarm*, gives us a visual of what happened to Satan's
dominion. As we have discussed earlier, Satan usurped Adam and
Eve's dominion through deception, and by their disobedience to
God's Word, he gained the title deed and became the god of this
world. The human race was brought into subjection to the hands of
the enemy. It would take a ransom of the highest price to redeem the
human race from his domain. Hebrews describes what Christ's death
did to Satan's control:

> Since the children have flesh and blood, he too
> shared in their humanity so that by his death
> he might break the power of him who holds
> the power of death—that is, the devil—and free
> those who all their lives were held in slavery by
> their fear of death (Hebrews 2:14–15, NIV)

---

[58] *Oxford Dictionary*. Copyright 1998, 2003, 2005, 2010. Oxford University
Press, Great Clarendon Street, Oxford, pg. 499

Now we see through the victory won by Christ's work that this loss of dominion (authority) has been reversed or rather restored to us through faith in his name. As believers, we no longer remain victims or subjects to the yoke of slavery to sin or Satan's realm. We are made victorious over sin and darkness. Through Christ's redemption in his blood, we are positioned on the finished side of the cross—the place of victory. That is why Christ stated, "All authority has been given to Me in heaven and on earth" (Matthew 28:18, NKJV).

This had been made official after his resurrection. He also says to John, "I am He who lives and was dead and behold I am alive forevermore. Amen. And I have the keys of Hades and of Death" (Revelation 1:18, NKJV). To have a set of keys means to have authority.

Jesus conquered Satan and all his dominion over our lives on our behalf.[59] In order for people to have this truth become a reality in their lives, they must hear and believe this good news, repent of their sinful deeds, accept Christ as Lord and Savior, and by this, each person can be saved through their personal decision. That is why we must share this good news to those who have not heard it. It is astounding to ponder that through our conscious choice to believe the Gospel, receiving Christ and his Lordship is what places us on the finished side of the cross. By surrendering our own will to Christ, we are made recipients of this blessed victory. Rick Renner wrote:

> Our view of spiritual warfare must begin with this basic understanding of Jesus's already accomplished victory over Satan. If we don't start out with this as our foundation, eventually we will be led to utterly ridiculous spiritual conclusions. The victory has already been won; there is nothing we can add to the destructive work Jesus did

[59] Kenyon, E. W. *What Happened from the Cross to the Throne.* Twenty-Sixth Printing. Copyright © 2010. Publisher: Kenyon's Gospel Publishing Society, Lynwood, WA. USA, pg. 65

to Satan's domain when He was raised from the dead.[60]

Having said all that, we can rest assured that because Christ did the conquering, we need only to stand in that victory. There is nothing that we need to do as an "extra" to gain an already accomplished victory over the devil. We are to simply stand in the authority in his name and we remain assertive against the enemy's tactics. The enemy knows he's been defeated, but it will not stop him from trying to work against God's people. However, he can only oppose as a usurper and not as one having dominion over spiritually born-again believers in Christ. The only authority he has is what we give him. If we believe his lies, such as the false notion of the "spiritual jurisdiction view," or yielding our flesh to sin, then he is able have access into our lives. Even so, the moment we repent and submit ourselves to God, the devil's power becomes defeated, "Submit to God. Resist the devil and he will flee from you" (James 4:7, NKJV).

When does it become defeated? Immediately.[61]

These principles of overcoming the devil have much to do with our personal lives. We cannot do this for others unless those with whom we share the Gospel choose to believe the message, and by their choice, we are able to cast out the evil spirits that have kept them bound. We can stand together in agreement for deliverance from sin and sickness in his name.

We also must realize that we cannot assume that we can take authority over spiritual darkness in "heavenly atmospheres" over regions. It is unfortunate that the "spiritual jurisdiction view" supposes that we have the power to do so. However, as we have observed, unless one has believed the Gospel, they will remain under Satan's

[60] Renner, Rick, *Dressed to Kill—A Biblical Approach to Spiritual Warfare and Armor.* Copyright 1991 by Rick Renner. Paperback Edition 2014, Third Printing. Publisher: Harrison House, Tulsa, OK. 74145, pg. 23

[61] Renner, Rick. *Dressed to Kill—A Biblical Approach to Spiritual Warfare and Armor.* Copyright 1991 by Rick Renner. Paperback Edition 2014, Third Printing. Publisher: Harrison House, Tulsa, OK 74145, pp. 42–45

domain. Again, the moment that an individual believes the Gospel is when they are delivered from his authority.

We must teach new believers that because of their choice to surrender to Christ, Satan's dominion over them has been nullified, "For sin shall no longer have dominion over you" (Romans 6:14a, NKJV). We must also teach new believers how to renew their mind in the truths of redemption, who they are in Christ, and that they are no longer victims. We must also teach that as believers, we have authority not in our own strength or identity but only in the name of Jesus. "In My name they will cast out demons…" (Mark 16:17c, NKJV).

6

Authority to Pray Based on Our
Righteousness in Christ

[t]he prayer of a righteous person is powerful and effective.

—James 5:16b, NIV

Upon reading the latter part of James 5:16 at one time, the writer felt immediately defeated, because the writer did not sense that she had yet attained that righteousness with God, even though she had been a believer after several years. This revealed a lack of teaching in light of what it means to be righteous. As the writer began to study what righteousness is, this verse of scripture, James 5:16, is now understood in a new light. To understand this verse is to understand the position we as believers in Christ hold in the place of prayer, and that is we are made his righteousness.

In light of what the author addresses as we look at this scripture in James, there is no indication of the need for a local representative to validate the prayer of the one who prays in Jesus's name. What James 5:16 presents to us is that effective prayer is made of that of a righteous person; it is the prayer of the one who is righteous.

To be righteous is to be in right standing with God based on his righteousness as we are in Christ. Being in Christ means that we are in his righteousness. Therefore, we can conclude that effective prayer is not conditional to a "gatekeeper" or a "host" as the "spiritual juris-diction view" claims; neither is it dependent upon our being native of a certain region. Rather, what authenticates effective prayer is in conjunction to the righteousness we have in Christ.

Often, we make assumptions that believers in general under-stand what righteousness means. Perceptions of being righteous vary in numerous churches and denominations. However, looking at the biblical concept about righteousness brings clarity when you under-stand biblical redemption.

Righteousness defined in light of redemption—E. W. Kenyon gives a brief definition on righteousness:

> We understand that Righteousness means the ability to stand in the Father's presence without the sense of guilt or inferiority.[62]

Being in his righteousness has nothing to do with our earthly accoutrements. Being in his righteousness enables our prayers to be heard. Righteousness enables us to have fellowship with God and our ability to commune with him. This righteousness was the very trait of that which man was originally created with as we read in the account of Genesis 1:26–27 in that we were made in the image of God.

Adam and Eve were able to stand in the Father's presence with-out any sense of guilt or inferiority. That is what it was to them to be righteous. This kind of righteousness was lost to the human race when our first ancestors disobeyed God, thereby subjecting man-kind under the curse of the law of sin and death, becoming slaves to unrighteousness (see Romans 5:12). Every human being from that point was born separated from God, dead in sin (unrighteousness), and under the domain of Satan's kingdom of darkness.[63]

---

[62] Kenyon, E. W. *Two Kinds of Righteousness—The Most Important Message Ever Offered to the Church*. Copyright 2011. Twenty-Fifth Printing, Kenyon's Gospel Publishing Society, INC. Lynwood, WA. 98046-0973, pg. 12

[63] Kenyon, E. W. *Two Kinds of Righteousness—The Most Message Ever Offered to the Church*. Copyright 2011. Kenyon's Gospel Publishing Society. Lynwood, WA.

Every human being would be born with a lack of righteous-ness, thereby giving Satan legal rights to hold us in bondage to sin. However, God is the only one who could provide a solution for our dilemma.

This righteousness is the very thing that Christ in the new cov-enant came to restore to mankind by reconciling us to God and once again reunited with his Spirit. We understand that God intended to restore humanity back to the original state that the image of himself (his righteousness) would be recreated in the human heart.

Since we have faith in Christ, we have become born again, which has made us a new creation. This fundamental truth is crucial to our right standing with God the Father. Faith in his Son alone, not in anything of ourselves, is where we rest. By this, we receive his righteousness. Without this, we have no privilege to petition God (see Appendix D).

Again, effective prayer is of that one who has received his righ-teousness in Christ by faith. As believers, we can, like Jesus, come before God and know that our prayers will be heard as we pray in Jesus's name.

Knowing our righteousness gives us godly confidence.

Paul reminds the Colossian believers "it is Christ in you the hope of glory" (Colossians 1:27b, NKJV). Christ in us is the hope that this world needs. Marie Brown shares the following on under-standing our righteousness:

> When we understand our righteousness, we begin to realize the responsibility and authority that God entrusts to us as an heir or son. It is from that position of our righteousness through Christ that we stand in a place of authority to do the works of God daily.[64]

98046-0973, pg. 23

[64] Brown, Marie. *Possessing Your Inheritance—Living in Your Righteousness.* Copyright 2007 by H. Marie Brown. Publisher: Marie Brown Ministries, Inc. Tulsa, OK. 74170, pg. 41

As we read through the book of Acts, we see the first century church in action. We observe these early believers as those who truly walked in spiritual authority as they were sent by God into several regions not of their descent. They did not wait for a welcoming committee or a "gatekeeper," nor did they wait for a special performance to give them a sign that they were welcomed to preach the Gospel. In fact, in several places, we read how it was the Holy Spirit who sent them.

At other times, he directed them not to go to certain places. They were simply led by the Holy Spirit as they also walked in a revelation of who they were in Christ. They preached no other message than the Gospel of Truth. We can also observe that it was at the preaching of the Gospel that whole societies were revolutionized for the glory of God. God confirmed the Word of the Gospel, not the word of man. He confirmed the preaching of the Gospel with his power, not because they distinguished their natural birth identity, but simply to make the name of Jesus known in all the places the Lord sent them.

Although they experienced intense persecution and opposition, they moved in a great anointing, not because of their claim to what they were in their racial or gender identity. They understood it was God's sending and God's empowerment. Upon observing this, these questions come to mind: Why can't we in the Western church see that? Do we not see how the early church exemplified this truth for us? Why are we complicating things? Do we not have the faith to walk in simple faith and obedience to do the Lord's bidding? Do we like popular opinion and prefer being illustrious for our natural birth identity? Are we afraid of persecution? Do we fear man? Why do we prefer the praise of man over the Word of God? Why do we respect the name of a person over the person of Jesus Christ and the revelation of him? Today, we want the signs, wonders, and miracles, yet we neglect preaching the Word of Truth—the Gospel that will change lives.

Today, there is excess of the word of man and not the word of God; then we wonder why we are powerless and not able to influence our own societies. We have become caught up with entertaining and appealing to the emotions of souls and the self-made images of our culture. We have made our own kind of Jesus from the imaginations of our own desires and have not learned to identify with the new creation in Christ that we are.

It is alarming that today the message of the redemption has become replaced by a lukewarm message with false prophetic inclinations. This results in many remaining ignorant of their redemption in Christ and their deliverance from bondage to sin. They remain bound and continue on living in patterns of sin. Many are misinformed about what it means to be the righteousness of God in Christ Jesus and misappropriate spiritual authority.

However, this does not have to stay this way if we as God's people return to the message of redemption as we learn from this central truth how to apply our spiritual authority in Christ.

7

Authority to Pray and Witness Based on Christ's Work

All believers in Christ are bestowed equal privilege to pray and to also minister to others in his name, because they are in his righteousness. Our right to minister through prayer is not dependent upon being from a certain locale, denomination, gender, tribe, or race. The Bible does not teach that being from a specific place or being a "gatekeeper" warrants more authority to minister in his name above others who are not native to their same location. All believers are included in the task of continuing the ministry of Jesus in every place to which he has sent each one. Kenneth E. Hagin wrote:

> All authority that was given to Christ belongs to us through him and we exercise it. We help him by carrying out his work on the earth. And one aspect of his work that the Word of God tells us to do is to stand our ground against the devil and put him on the run with the Word. In fact, Christ can't do his work on earth without us![65]

---

[65] Hagin, Kenneth E. *The Believer's Authority*. The Believer's Authority, Legacy Edition. Copyright 1967, 1986, 2004, 2009. Rhema Bible Church. Electronic

To suggest that original authority is given to those "host people"—gatekeepers (those whose birth origin from a certain location)—is to exclude the remaining body of believers and limit Christ's authority within each one. Authority over the powers of darkness is based on the authority which Christ granted in his name to every believer.[66] Understanding our position that we are in his righteousness through faith in Christ, we will begin to appropriate the finished work of Christ. Knowing what was accomplished in his work reveals to us the standing in Christ, which we hold.

The foundation, which this author seeks to establish regarding true spiritual authority in this volume, is that which Christ has done for us. It is therefore brought to the attention of the reader to show that being born in the natural from a certain location does not give one more spiritual authority in their birthplace. To say that a "move of God" is dependent upon the "host" people of their native land is when the forces of hell will be defeated when they begin to arise is to say that "outsiders" who are sent to them are unauthorized. This limits Christ's authority within all believers. By doing this, we negate Jesus's own declaration—"It is finished!"—from the cross.

However, those who know their righteousness in Christ, regardless of their natural birth identity, are those who will do the works of righteousness, and that includes prayer and ministering the Gospel.

With this in mind, the writer will highlight a few observations regarding spiritual warfare as this is in keeping with a believer's right to minister the Gospel as an act of spiritual warfare. T. L. Osborn wrote:

Paul spoke of helping together by prayer (2Cor.1:11). He was on the front lines and needed

Edition Published 2010, a.k.a. Kenneth Hagin Ministries, Inc. Chapter 5, pg. 105

[66] Kenyon, E. W. *Two Kinds of Righteousness—The Most Important Message Ever Offered to the Church.* Twenty-fifth Printing. Copyright 2011. Publisher: Kenyon's Gospel Publishing Society, Lynwood, WA. 98046-0973, pg. 24

the Christians to help him in prayer. Prayer for what? He urged the believers in Thessalonica to pray that the Word of the Lord MIGHT HAVE FREE COURSE (2 Th.3:1). Why? So that the gospel would not be hindered by society's political and governmental rulers of darkness in high places, nor be rejected by the people. Paul did not engage the Christians to pull the stronghold of the rulers of darkness by prayer. They had no authority to demand Satan's surrender so believers could impose the Christian faith. To bring Christ's salvation to the un-converted, Paul knew he must inform the Enemy's subjects of the gospel which is the power of God unto salvation (Rom. 1:16). Paul knew that if he could do that effectively, his gospel witness would have free course and the people would hear it and believe it. When they did that, Satan's strongholds would be pulled down and his rule over their lives would be ended because Satan cannot hold people captive against their will to receive Jesus Christ as Lord.[67]

On the subject of spiritual warfare, the writer thought it noteworthy to highlight Kenneth E. Hagin's insight on the context of Ephesians 6:12:

> By overemphasizing just one verse alone over the whole counsel of God, people place emphasis not on what Christ has already done for believers, but rather on what the Christian must yet do in order to get victory over the devil. This is

---

[67] Osborn, T. L. *The Message that Works*. Copyright 2004 by LaDonna C. Osborn. Publisher: Osborn Publishers, Tulsa, OK. 74102, USA, pp. 254–255

unscriptural because every believer already participates in Jesus's victory over Satan.[68]

There is nothing more to do as far as gaining victory. Rather, we rest on what Christ has done and enforce the victory we have gained in Christ. Every believer in every location, no matter their race, tribe, gender, or origin of birth is given equal duty to minister in the authority of Jesus's name in all the places he sends each one. Highlighting what T. L. Osborn also wrote:

> Each Christian's calling is to give witness of the gospel to un-believers—to captives of the rulers of darkness...Christians do not struggle against this defeated foe on our own terrain where Jesus is Lord. Those who have embraced Christ as Savior and Lord are redeemed. Believers engage Satan out on his own territory—out where he is bent on ruling the minds and lives of people. Believers fight to make known the Good News among Satan's slaves. They fight to penetrate his curtain of darkness, to get the attention of un-believers, to make Christ's message known to them, and to convince them of the gospel message. The believer's ministry is witness of Christ's death, burial, resurrection and ascension. It is making the significance of those events known to the un-converted (Acts 1:8; 5:32).[69]

It is crucial that we never shift from the central truth that it is in his name that we have spiritual authority. Again, we do not have

---

[68] Hagin, Kenneth E. *The Triumphant Church.* Copyright 1993. Rhema Bible Church. Electronic Edition Published 2010, a.k.a. Kenneth Hagin Ministries Inc., Chapter 8

[69] Osborn, T. L. *The Message that Works.* Copyright 2004 by LaDonna C. Osborn. Publisher: Osborn Publishers, Tulsa, OK. 74102, USA, pp. 220, 288–289

spiritual authority in our own identity, be it racial, gender, or birth origin. In his name, we are authorized to minister to people and to petition God. This spiritual authority that we have in his name is not conditional to the geographical location of our birth origin. In his book, *The Name of Jesus*, Kenneth E. Hagin wrote:

> In the Name of Jesus! He authorized us. He gave us his Name as the authority. The power is in the Name. The authority is in the Name. He gave us the Name that is recognized in three worlds—the Name that has authority in heaven, on earth, and under the earth. Angels, men, and demons have to bow at that Name—and that Name belongs to us. We are authorized to use that Name.[70]

Author Daisy Washburn-Osborn also wrote touching the concept of equal opportunity for every believer. As she addresses women, the principle she brings forth pertains not only to gender issues but also to racial, tribal, or social issues. The author of this thesis deemed it noteworthy to bring to light:

> Jesus explained it all when He said: 'The thief (Satan) comes only to steal, and to kill, and to destroy' (John 10:10). But God is not willing that any should perish, but that all should come to repentance (2 Pe. 3:9). You, as a woman, were not born to be a slave, but to be an heir of God, a joint-heir with Jesus Christ (Rom. 8:16–17; Gal. 3:29).—to be God's friend and partner. You see, God is Spirit. You as a woman, are his flesh. Whatever He does, He does it through his body—his church, which is people—ordinary

---

[70] Hagin, Kenneth E. *The Name of Jesus*, Legacy Edition. Copyright 1979, 2006, 2007. Rhema Bible Church. Electronic Edition Published 2010, a.k.a. Kenneth Hagin Ministries, Inc., Chapter 6

women and men like you and me (1 Co. 3:16, 6:19; Eph. 2:21).[71]

All believers are anointed to pray. How do we know we have been anointed to pray? How do we know we have the anointing? What is the anointing?

> The anointing which you have received from him abides in you, and you do not need that anyone teach you; but as the same anointing teaches you concerning all things, and is true and is not a lie, and just as it has taught you, you will abide in him. (1 John 2:27, NKJV)

Anointing defined from *Strong's* derived from 1 John 2:7: an unguent or smearing, i.e. (figuratively) the special endowment ("chrism") of the Holy Spirit.[72]

Jesus taught that the role of the Holy Spirit to every believer was that he would be our teacher, our helper, comforter, and our advocate (John 14:15,26, 15:26, 16:7,12). He also taught that his Holy Spirit would dwell in us. As he sends us, we receive this special endowment for the task to which he has called us to. We can also rest assured that because Jesus is the source of truth (John 14:6), then his Holy Spirit will keep us in truth. His Holy Spirit is the essence of the indwelling anointing—special endowment—by which we as believers are empowered to minister to a hurting world to make disciples of all nations. His role in our lives also helps us to discern false doctrine. John, therefore, exhorted believers about

---

[71] Osborn, Daisy Washburn. *The Woman Believer*. Copyright 1990. Publisher: OSFO Publishers, Tulsa, OK. 74102, USA, pp. 141–142

[72] Strong's word number: g5545. χρίσμα chrisma; from 5548: *Olive Tree Enhanced Strong's Dictionary*. Copyright 1998–2017. Olive Tree Bible Software

this anointing we have within. *Expositor's Bible Commentary* gives this insight:

> These verses encourage believers to pass the test and cling to the rule of faith so that they are not "[led] astray." Everything they need to know has been provided by the "anointing," the true gospel they have already received, which teaches them "all things." Those who suggest that they have something to offer beyond this teaching are therefore deceivers. Of course, the Antichrists did not think of themselves in this way, and John is probably referring to their doctrine rather than their motives. They would insist that their views are a legitimate extension of what John taught. John therefore emphasizes that the anointing is "real, not counterfeit"; nothing can be true that is not consistent with it. Orthodox tradition must be the standard for measuring new revelations and personal spiritual experience.[73]

The above reference has been included as we are considering the aspect about the anointing for the purpose of the misgivings that there has been regarding the anointing. The scruple is that special persons, such as the "host people" or "gatekeepers," are anointed specifically for their territory. However, when a proper understanding of redemption is in place, one will no longer be misguided by erroneous teaching about the anointing or spiritual authority.

The anointing is not an object that we possess; rather, the anointing is a person, the very presence of the Spirit of God residing within all believers to be his witnesses. It is due to this truth that we can appreciate that we have equal opportunity with other believers in Christ. In light of understanding the anointing within us, we can

---

[73] *Expositor's Bible Commentary.* 1 John 2:26–27 (13 vol. series). Copyright 1998–2017. Olive Tree Bible Software

then begin to reconcile that this anointing to minister the Gospel is not limited to an "elect" group of believers. Rather, all believers who are in obedience to Christ have equal anointing to minister the Gospel. "Christ in you the hope of glory" (Colossians 1:27, NKJV). In his book, *Understanding the Anointing*, Kenneth E. Hagin wrote:

> Every believer has anointing-an unction-that abides within him, because the Holy Spirit comes in us in the New Birth. Romans 8:9 says, 'Now if any man have not the Spirit of Christ, he is none of his.' The Spirit of Christ is the Holy Spirit.[74]

We can walk in purposeful confidence, knowing that God has chosen each of us to be his voice, his hands, and feet as his anointed vessels to reach this hurting world with his love. We are challenged to throw off the limitations of faddish teachings, such as the "spiritual jurisdiction view" and other types of tradition which this world has placed on us. Christ has come to set us free to be all that God has designed and called us to be. We can help others become free from the limits that have been placed upon them as well by helping them discover their righteousness in Christ, which is the foundation of walking in true spiritual authority.

---

[74] Hagin, Kenneth E. *Understanding the Anointing*. Copyright 1983. Rhema Bible Church. Electronic Edition Published 2013, a.k.a. Kenneth Hagin Ministries Inc., Chapter 2

8

The Proper Spiritual Clothing—
The Value of Our Identity in Christ

This volume has been addressing what the author has termed a Spiritual Jurisdiction View. The author believes that this notion has brought about a false perception of the believer's significance to their natural birth identity as it breeds the misconception regarding the basis of our spiritual authority.

We have discussed so far the importance of being born again, our redeemed status, a study on biblical equality in light of redemption, and what it means for all believers to be included in his covenant. We have also discussed the source of our spiritual authority—our righteousness in Christ—enabling our privilege to pray in Jesus's name. As the "spiritual jurisdiction view" is being addressed, we can understand that the initial problem of this view is due to a lack of understanding of our redeemed identity in Christ.

We will focus on aspects of the spiritual birth identity—the birth that counts—that when grasped, believers will be liberated with a renewed confidence to continue the ministry of Christ in this hurting world. We will now view the source of our true identity in Christ from the beginning of man's creation and what Jesus's sacrifice means in restoring this lost identity to us.

Our Original Covering

Let us make man in our image, according to our likeness...

And the Lord God formed the man of the dust of the ground and breathed into his nostrils the breath of life; and man became a living being. (Genesis 1:26a, 2:7, NKJV)

This scripture speaks to us of mankind's original God-designed identity. This original identity was sourced in the life and spirit connection to God our Creator of which man was formerly created. Genesis 1:26 reveals that mankind was made in the image of God. We often wonder, what did that look like? As God our Creator breathed into man the breath of life, man became a living being, thereby being created in union with him. Adam was the first human being who received an impartation, a deposit of his Spirit. Man, therefore, is a spirit created by God who is Spirit. John R. Cross gives a clear perception on the word's breath of life:

The words 'breath of life' are often associated with the spirit or non-material side of man. This is an additional reflection of God's image, for God is Spirit. As we stated before, spirits cannot be seen since they have no bodies. However, in man's case, God chose to provide a physical house of flesh and bones for man's spirit to dwell in—a house formed from the dust of the ground. Once formed, the body would have laid there, complete in every way, but entirely lifeless. It was when God breathed into the spirit of man, that the body became alive. Only God can impart life; no person or angel has that ability.[75]

---

[75] Cross, John R. *The Stranger on the Road to Emmaus*. Edition 5a, Copyright 2014, Publisher: GoodSeed International, Olds AB, T4H 1P5, pp 42–43

This impartation was the very nature of God himself. Man was created in the nature of God's righteousness—his image. Being created in his righteousness, this also became a covering which enabled him to stand in the presence of God the Father without the sense of guilt, fear, shame, or inferiority. God's Spirit was man's original covering, a covering of righteousness.

The very identity of the first created man and woman was that they were formed as children of God who resembled his character. His very image was expressed through their lives.

They had unbroken fellowship with their Creator as he was also their best friend. There were many combining factors to their original state: They were made in the image of God, they were one with him by his Spirit, and they were clothed in his righteousness. As friends of God, they were able to communicate with him on an intellectual and spiritual level. In his book, *The Hidden Man*, E. W. Kenyon wrote:

> You understand that man is in God's class of being. When he was created in the Garden he was made in the image of God and likeness of God. He had to be a spirit being because God is Spirit. He was created so that, by partaking of God's nature, he might become a child of God. If he were but a physical being he could not receive the nature of God's nature. If he were but a mental being, he could not receive God's nature. He had to be a spirit being, an eternal being who would live as long as God lives. Man had to be in God's class. He had to be created so that he could be the companion and associate of Deity.[76]

---

[76] Kenyon, E. W. *The Hidden Man—An Unveiling of the Subconscious Mind.* Copyright 2012. Twenty-Fourth Printing. Publisher: Kenyon's Gospel Publishing Services Inc, Lynnwood, Washington, pg. 7

In their original state, they had no sense of poverty. They were complete, whole, and secure in the One who created them.

> They were both naked, the man and his wife, and
> were not ashamed. (Genesis 2:25, NKJV)

This covering, being clothed in his righteousness, explains why they felt no need to be covered with anything else. They were complete in God's glorious presence. The sense of nakedness and shame was unknown to them. It was only until they disobeyed that insecurity replaced their sense of righteousness, shame replaced dignity, nakedness instead of his covering.

We will soon look into those dynamics. Before we do, we will examine the type of attire which Jesus illustrates in a parable in the book of Matthew. We will see how this relates to the concept of a covering; or rather, proper spiritual clothing that is needed for one to maintain the right to remain in the kingdom of God.

Jesus talked about the proper clothing. In summary, Matthew 22:1–14 relates a parable which Jesus taught to warn listeners about the importance of having the "proper clothing" in the kingdom of heaven. This kind of clothing spoke of a spiritual clothing. In this parable, he describes a wedding feast prepared by a king where many guests had been invited. Many of his invited guests were too occupied with their own lives to come to this wedding feast.

Therefore, a second invitation was extended to those in the highways and byways to come to this prepared wedding feast. The wedding hall was then filled with these guests. As he arrived at the hall to come and visit his guests, he noticed a man who did not have on a wedding garment. He reprimanded him for not coming properly dressed. This guest was speechless, and sadly, he was cast out.

One can read this passage of scripture and feel pity for the guest who had been banished. That sympathy evokes this kind of question: "What if he was poor and came in with his best clothes?" It doesn't seem fair. What was Jesus teaching from this parable? When we consider the context of the cultural customs during the time of the kings of the East, we learn that not only was appropriate dress required, it

THE BIRTH THAT COUNTS

was also provided to ensure that proper attire was worn. Jameison's Commentary explains:

> The custom in the East of presenting festival gar-
> ments (see Ge 45:22; 2Ki 5:22), even though nor
> clearly proved, is certainly presupposed here. It
> undoubtedly means something which they bring
> not of their own—for how could they have any
> such dress who were gathered in from the high-
> ways indiscriminately?—but which they receive
> as their appropriate dress. And what can that be
> but what is meant by "putting on the Lord Jesus,"
> as "THE LORD OUR RIGHTEOUSNESS?"
> (See Ps 45:13, 14).[77]

This noted commentary sheds light on the dynamics that occurred within the parable which Jesus related. The God's Word Translation states Matthew 22:11 in this fashion, "When the king came to see the guests, he saw a person who was not dressed in the wedding clothes provided for the guests."

Through this, we bridge the wedding account to the account in Genesis chapters three and four, for it holds the same principle—the proper garments were provided by the king. Before we discuss this parable further, we need to look again at what those dynamics were in the Genesis account regarding the concept of covering or rather proper clothing.

God Provided a Covering

We have discussed earlier about the high treason of Adam not only with the consequences of losing dominion as the "god" of this world to the deceiver Satan, but mankind also lost a crucial part to

---

[77] Jameison, Faussett, and Brown Commentary. Matthew 22:11. Copyright 1998–2017. Olive Tree Bible Software

their identity. Righteousness was lost, which in effect was their original covering. Let's look at this original covering of righteousness.

First of all, Genesis chapter one reveals the creation of all things, including the creation of mankind. Our first ancestors—Adam and Eve—were originally made in the image of God, after his likeness. He had given them a deposit of his Spirit, and his righteous holy nature defined who they were. This enabled them to always be in his presence.

Genesis chapter two reveals that they had no shame. The reason for this is that they were covered with the glory of God as he was their initial covering. They held an incredible union with God's Spirit. He was their source of life. They had unbroken fellowship with God. To summarize, Genesis chapter three records the account of their disobedience to God as they were instructed by him not to eat of the tree of knowledge of good and evil. We have learned that the serpent (Satan) succeeds in deceiving them by causing them to doubt God's word, and eventually, they disobeyed God's Word. Their disobedience had immediate ramifications.

Immediately, they recognized their nakedness, an indication that their original spiritual covering was removed. That spiritual dynamic became realized as their sin separated them from God's Spirit, and they no longer were covered by his glory. In attempt to make up for this dilemma, they made fig leaves to cover their shame. However, their own self-made covering did not remedy the inner bareness which they had begun to sense within.

In fear, they ran from God when they heard him walking in the garden. They never felt fear before. Neither had they ever felt shame. They never knew what it was to be uncovered. Tragically, their act of treason had sold themselves over to Satan, being subject to bondage to sin. Consequently, they no longer had their original covering—their original identity—the righteous and holy nature of God. Instead, they became filled with a sin nature. In place of a righteous consciousness, a sin consciousness became their new reality, which incited a dread of God's presence.

This truly was a devastating moment. The very thing that God warned them about was that they would die if they disobeyed.

Though they did not die immediately in the physical sense, they first died spiritually as eventually, their bodies would give way to physical death. They had become disconnected from their source of life.

The second death would come later in that when they died physically; their souls would also become separated from their bodies and from God forever in the lake of fire. Romans 6:23 reminds us that the wages of sin is death. However, God did not leave them helpless. It would take death for them to pay for their sin debt. It could not be the death of just anything, but it had to be something innocent. Adam and Eve could not pay for their sin with their own death, because they were no longer innocent of sin.

God had to be the one who provided a covering for them. An atonement. Genesis 3:21 reveals how God made tunics of skin to cover both Adam and Eve. Therefore, the shed blood of this innocent animal would be their substitute, and atonement would be made for them to signify that a covering was made for them. By this, we learn that their own coverings of fig leaves did not remedy their problem of lost righteousness—their lost covering. Neither could these fig leaves recover their original identity.

The covering which God made was the only solution to make them acceptable in his presence. However, this atonement was a temporary covering; yet, it did not change their spiritual condition. The sad truth was that innocent blood had to be shed in order for them to be clothed.

Obviously, God did not accept the covering which they made for themselves—fig leaves. God showed them what would be acceptable. He provided atonement, a right type of covering, yet it took the shedding of the blood of an innocent animal. John R. Cross explains:

> Just as Adam and Eve could not make themselves acceptable to God by fixing up their outward appearance, neither can we be accepted based on our externals.
>
> We may impress others with what we are on the outside, but God knows what we are really like. We saw that God provided Adam and Eve

with a way of acceptance, but on different terms. The Bible says that, 'The Lord God made garments of skin for Adam and his wife and clothed them' (Gen. 3:21). The significance of this little verse would be overlooked if it wasn't' for other parts of the Bible explaining it. So, what does it mean? What would Jesus have told the disciples? Very simply this: Just as an animal had to die to clothe Adam and Eve in acceptable clothing, so Jesus had to die to make us acceptable in the presence of God.[78]

God in his wisdom knew what it would take to restore righteousness to us. Nothing of this world would compensate for what is truly missing. Through redemption in his blood, our true identity, our self-worth is restored. By his blood, we are properly clothed in a spiritual sense. We have restored relationship with God through Jesus Christ. As a result, our true covering in Christ is also restored, which also indicates the recovery of our true identity. In his book, *God's Love Plan*, T. L. Osborn wrote:

> God is love and love never quits. his love went into action the day Adam and Eve broke confidence with him. He found a legal way to restore humankind back to an intimate relationship with him.[79]

Two sacrifices were made—one was accepted, one was rejected. Remember in Genesis chapter four how Cain and Abel made a sacrifice to God? Whose sacrifice was accepted? Whose sacrifice was

---

[78] Cross, John R. *The Stranger on the Road to Emmaus*. Edition 5a. Copyright 2014. Publisher: GoodSeed International, Olds AB, T4H 1P5, pg. 233

[79] Osborn, T. L. *God's Love Plan*. Copyright 1984. Publisher: OSFO BOOKS, OSFO INTERNATIONAL, Osborn Publishers, Tulsa, OK. 74102, USA, pg. 87

rejected? As we read the account, we find that Abel's sacrifice was accepted, and Cain's was rejected. Why was this so? Cain offered his best. He picked the best of the produce he had grown from the ground, and yet he was rejected. This too did not seem fair.

Did God not see that it was his best? By his actions, Cain revealed that he did not trust God's way of atonement. Produce, herbs, or anything grown of earth does not shed blood. Abel's sacrifice was accepted because he offered what God required. Abel offered an innocent and spotless male animal from his herd and offered its fat on the altar. This was the right kind of sacrifice as it provided atonement for Abel crediting to him righteousness, enabling him to maintain his relationship with God.

We need to think this through. If Cain offered the same as his brother, Abel, would God have accepted him? What did Cain do? He trusted in his own wisdom and offered what he thought would be good enough. However, it did not provide atonement, thereby positioning him as not being in right standing with God.

As orchestrated by God, only through the shedding of blood was the way that covering was provided. It was God who showed the way. Mankind was taught this from the beginning that in order to maintain their relationship with God, they would have to make a substitute offering according to the standards that God originally taught Adam and Eve.

Leviticus 17:11 reiterates, "For the life of the flesh is in the blood, and I have given it to you upon the altar to make atonement for your souls; for it is the blood that makes atonement for the soul" (NKJV). This practice of the blood sacrifice for atonement was continually observed throughout the Old Testament among God's people.

God's Way Is Best

Throughout the Old Testament, we learn that God had established a covenant with his people. In order to maintain their relationship with God and to be accepted by God, they would have to make an atonement offering. By this, they portrayed their trust in God by coming to God through his way—through the blood sacrifice. His covenant (agreement) with his people was sealed through the shed blood of the sacrificial lamb, and atonement was made.

Things were done this way throughout the Old Testament. But God's people did not always continue in their agreement with him. They went astray and worshipped false gods. They practiced wrong rituals which God did not teach. They also blended ungodly practices from false religions with the sacrifices to God. They combined these ungodly practices with all kinds of immorality, idolatry, and witchcraft. They had become corrupt and had gone their own way.

Why was that? Why is that God's people could not keep their agreement? It wasn't God's fault. He had shown them the acceptable way. Why then could they not continue in his way?

Let's take this question further: Why is this world in a mess today? Ever since Adam and Eve, mankind has been born with a sin nature. That sin nature always leads mankind to walk away from God and do their own thing. Because of Adam and Eve's disobedience, a curse was unleashed on the whole of creation. As we read in Romans 5:12, "Therefore, just as through one man, sin entered the world, and death through sin, and thus death spread to all men" (NKJV).

Simply stated, sinful man has given birth to sinful man. From this time of the fall, the whole human race would be born in a sinful condition, separated from God, and with an innate knowledge that something is missing. What is missing? Righteousness, which is man's covering, their original identity. Religions all over the earth try to supplement the missing piece and to no avail; all efforts are not enough. Nothing of this world can recover what was lost in the garden.

The record of Adam and Eve's attempt to cover themselves with fig leaves reveals the beginnings of mankind looking to nature to resolve their problem. This is the core of false religion.

Only God knew how to solve this dilemma. The scriptures reveal prophecies regarding the new heart, the new creation, and the new identity as foretold by both Jeremiah and Ezekiel (Jeremiah 31:33–34; Ezekiel 36:25–29). King David prayed for this new heart as he realized his sinful condition. He is the only King of Israel to actually come to this realization as we read his prayer of repentance in Psalm 51. "Create in me a clean heart O' God and renew a right spirit within me" (Psalm 51:10, NKJV). David knew that he needed an inward change, a condition that no amount of sacrifices could do for him. Yet, he cried out for it.

Back to the conversation between Jesus and Nicodemus, he clarifies the time of fulfillment of the promise given back in the Garden of Eden had come to pass. God said to Eve that he would raise up a seed that would deliver mankind from Satan's rule and crush his dominion over them (see Genesis 3:15). That seed, from that point, would be known as the promised deliverer, namely the Messiah.

The time had come, and Nicodemus was yet to see it happen. Jesus said to him, "For God so loved the world that He gave his only begotten Son that whoever believes in him will not die but have everlasting life. For God did not send his Son into the World to condemn the world but that the world through him might be saved" (John 3:16–17, NKJV). He was teaching Nicodemus the importance of believing in his Son in order to become born again as this was conditional to being accepted in his kingdom. His natural birth or religious observance did not help to give him this right or make him acceptable in the kingdom of God. His good works did not grant him righteousness. The writer to the Hebrews wrote:

> But Christ became as High Priest of the good things to come, with the greater and more perfect tabernacle not made with hands, not of this creation. (Hebrews 9:11, NKJV)

It is made clear, "[n]ot made with hands, not of this creation." Nothing of this world including our natural birth identity and including our cultural accoutrements could even come close to bridging the gap or make us acceptable to God. Adam and Eve's fig leaves were not acceptable either. The Hebrew writer goes on to say:

> Not with the blood of goats and calves, but with his own blood He entered the Most Holy

115

Place once for all, having obtained eternal redemption…

How much more shall the blood of Christ, who through the eternal Spirit offered Himself without spot to God, cleanse your conscience from dead works to serve the living God? (Hebrews 9:12,14, NKJV)

It is only through the atonement that Christ made which enables all who believe to be made right with God. However, the sacrifice of Jesus provides for us more than atonement, being that we are more than forgiven. As we said earlier that in this new covenant, by being born again, we are made a new creation, "For if any man be in Christ, he is a new creation, old things are passed away behold all things are made new" (2 Cor. 5:17, NKJV). The unfolding aspect of being made a new creation is to receive a new spiritual identity, a spiritual clothing of righteousness.

Revelations speaks of a great multitude in heaven standing before God's throne as having been "clothed with white robes" (Revelations 7:9, NKJV). There is no other identified color in their robes since they have been made white as this was symbolic of spiritual purity, because their sins were away washed in the Lamb's blood. This was also symbolic of one common identity in that they had become the redeemed of the Lord who gathered to lift up their voice, saying, "Salvation belongs to God who sits on the throne and to the Lamb" (Revelations 7:10, NKJV).

The Connection to the Wedding Feast

Returning to the wedding feast, we started in this section observing the Matthew 22:1–14 reference. Now we understand this part of the wedding feast parable. The invitation to the wedding had been sent out toward many throughout the land. The first group to receive the invitation was too occupied with their lives. As a result, the invitation was sent to many others among the highways and byways.

As stated earlier, in those days, it was the king that provided the garments. The king in this parable represents God himself. Here we make the connection. There are those who when they accept the invitation have put on the garments which were provided for each of them. They are likened to Abel who appropriated the right kind of sacrifice for atonement. Then there are those that accept the invitation but refuse to wear the garments provided. Like Cain, they feel they can come of their own preference in their own clothing, their own identity. This speaks of those who want to continue to identify with their old life, with the world, their own ways, their own philosophy, and whatever else they have been brought up with.

The question we are faced with is: Was this guest who also accepted the invitation, as he came in his own clothing, accepted by the king in this parable? We find the unfortunate answer in Matthew 22:12–13: "So he said to him, 'Friend, how did you come in here without a wedding garment?' And he was speechless. 'Bind him hand and foot and cast him into outer darkness where there will be weeping and gnashing of teeth'" (NKJV).

Obviously, Jesus is speaking of a spiritual wedding feast with a forewarning not to assume that even though you accept the invitation, you must also identify with the covering he provides by wearing it. Look at the King's heart. He called him friend. He must have felt hurt that this guest would not accept the wedding garments provided by the King himself. You can feel his disappointment. He talked to him respectfully; however, this guest was not accepted. Why? He did not wear the garments that the King provided. His actions were like Cain's. He must have thought to himself, *The king will accept me as I am. After all, he is a loving king. He gave me an invitation.*

He did not realize that he insulted the King by not being properly clothed. He was then cast out into outer darkness. May we never make the same mistake.

The wedding feast is not about us, but it is about King Jesus; Christianity is not about us, but it is about Christ.

This parable as told by Jesus, who is the King of heaven, Jesus the King, with his heart of love, warns us not to walk in our own self-righteousness, ways, and identity. We are taught by the lesson of the wedding feast parable that we are the ones who need to change. He made it possible for us to do so. He provided the right garments for us. These are the garments of righteousness—proper spiritual clothing.

We must adhere the principle of this parable and heed the warning to never assume that we can remain as we are and continue to identify with our former life before we accept the invitation to receive Christ. We are required by Jesus to deny ourselves, take up our cross, and follow him (see Mark 8:34b). We are to first of all deny ourselves our self. Understand that the walk of Christianity is no longer about us nor is it about our self-made identity. We no longer pursue the things of this world but Christ. "Seek ye first the kingdom of God and his righteousness" (Matthew 6:33, NKJV).

> "[p]ut on the new man who is renewed in knowl-
> edge according to the image of him who created
> him" (Colossians 3:10, NKJV)

His righteousness has been provided for us through the atoning sacrifice of his Son. His blood was shed on our behalf for our redemption, reconciliation, and covering. This righteousness is imparted to us as we have faith in him alone, "it shall be imputed to us who believe in him who raised up Jesus our Lord from the dead" (Romans 4:24, NKJV).

The Robe of Righteousness

> I will greatly rejoice in the Lord, my soul shall be
> joyful in my God; for He has clothed me with the
> garments of salvation, He has covered me with
> the robe of righteousness. (Isaiah 61:10, NKJV)

It is a remarkable thing to grasp that God has covered us with the robe of righteousness as this scripture in Isaiah portrays the spiritual dynamics when the Lord clothed Adam and Eve by those garments of skin. It also points us to that which God does for those who look to Christ for redemption. E. W. Kenyon wrote:

> Man's being legally declared righteous in Christ made it possible for him to approach God through Christ to receive eternal life, God's nature. This is the second step in this revelation of righteousness. First, we were declared righteous, that is freed from the condemnation wrought by Adam's transgression. Second, when we accept Christ as Savior and Lord we become freed from all personal transgressions, we have imparted to us God's nature.
>
> Receiving God's nature is in reality receiving his righteousness. It was Christ's having our spiritual death laid upon him that made him sin, as unrighteous as we were. Now our receiving God's nature cause us to become his righteousness. 2 Cor. 5:21 reveals this fact: 'him who knew no sin He made to become sin on our behalf; that we might become the righteousness of God in him.' He became sin by receiving our nature; we become the righteousness of God by receiving his nature…
>
> Here is the secret of the power that you have been seeking in your life. It is in knowing that you are the righteousness of God. No longer will you be hindered in taking your place or using the authority of the Name of Jesus through which He will be glorified.[80]

---

[80] Kenyon, E. W. *The Father and His Family*. Twenty-Sixth Printing. Copyright 2013. Publisher: Kenyon's Gospel Publishing Society, Lynwood Washington, USA pp. 222, 224

Our redemption would not have been made possible if it were not for the shed blood of Christ. Based on his substitute sacrifice, his blood not only brings us forgiveness, but it also brings us total cleansing of all sin, and we are made righteous. As believers, we can conclude that our true identity is restored in that we have been made the righteousness of God in Christ Jesus through his blood.

> You must know (recognize) that you were redeemed (ransomed) from the useless (fruitless) way of living inherited by tradition from [your] forefathers, not with corruptible things [such as] silver and gold, But [you were purchased] with the precious blood of Christ (the Messiah), like that of a [sacrificial] lamb without blemish or spot. (1 Peter 1:18–19, AMPC)

The basis for the redemption of true spiritual identity is in the blood of Christ, making us citizens of the kingdom of God. As believers, we all share in one identity, we are the household of God, and we are brought into the new covenant. Since we have also received total remission of our sins, we also have received his righteousness in the new creation. Nothing of this world can measure up to the atoning sacrifice of Christ, neither can anything of this world add to what he has accomplished.

Understanding this truth enables all believers to walk in renewed in confidence based upon who they are in Christ. The writer is not saying that one should reject their native identity; but rather, our focus now as believers is about our restored identity in Christ. Christ restored our original spiritual identity to us. This is why he died, was buried, and rose again for us.

Our biological factors of who we are in the natural do not change, but our spiritual condition has been transformed upon our becoming born again by faith in Christ. Everything that we are now becomes identified with Christ. Since this is so, any ungodly accoutrements of our culture must surrender to the cross. Our expression of who we are is now about our faith in Christ.

Our natural identity cannot give added spiritual dynamic to our walking in spiritual authority. Since our natural birth could not help to change our spiritual condition of having a sin nature, it certainly doesn't empower our new life in Christ. Our newfound identity in Christ is the essence of who we are as believers, and by this, we have a new kind of confidence—a "Godfidence." We have been made the righteousness of God in Christ (see 2 Corinthians 5:21).

9

Identity Restored:
Christ Is Our New Identity

If any man be in Christ, he is a new creation, old things
are passed away, behold all things are made new.

—2 Corinthians 5:17, NKJV

I have been crucified with Christ; it is no longer I who live, but
Christ lives in me; and the life which in now live in the flesh I live
the faith in the son God who love me and gave Himself for me.

—Galatians 2:20, NKJV

In Christ, we have a new identity, a new purpose, a new vision, and a new life. We live no longer by the standards or pursuits of this world. We are no longer subject to cultural elements pertaining from our former upbringing. We no longer live by how we used to identify ourselves. Our past does not determine who we are. We are no longer products of our past. We are no longer products of the generational sins of our fathers. We no longer continue to live as people who are affected by intergenerational injustices. All of that is done away with in Christ. We can live in spiritual liberty, knowing that we are no longer victims or subjects to sin.

Jesus changed our history. We now identify with Christ. We now put on Christ. We live Christ. We pursue Christ. It is from that place that we as believers can pray, preach, and minister the gospel of Jesus Christ. In his book, *Now We Are in Christ*, Kenneth Copeland wrote:

> Being in Christ makes you a new creature, or a new creation. The literal Greek text says, 'a new species of being which never existed before.' When you became a new creature, your spirit is completely re-created. Old things are passed away, all things become new, and all things are of God.[81]

We must always reflect upon the new creation concept that this now defines who we are as believers. This is our new identity, who we are in Christ as a new creation. In his book, *What We Are in Christ*, E. W. Kenyon wrote:

> To most of us what we were before we found Christ so dominates our minds, so rules us that we forget what we are now in him. We belittle our Redemption and we magnify our failures. Our weakness is ever with us. We have forgotten that He is ever with us. We have a 'Cross' religion, rather than the resurrected life of the Son of God. If we would persistently fix our thoughts upon what we are in Christ and what Christ is doing for us at the right of the Father, it would lift us out of weakness and failure, into his strength...The New Creation is a part of God. It

---

[81] Copeland, Kenneth. *Now We Are in Christ Jesus.* Copyright 1980. Eagle Mountain International Church, Incorporated, a.k.a. Kenneth Copeland Ministries. Publisher: Kenneth Copeland Publications, Fort Worth, TX. 76192-0001 pg. 25

has partaken of God's nature. It has been made out of Righteousness and holiness of truth. The New Creation is not a man-made thing. It is not a mental thing. It is a thing of God. Just as the angel said, Lk. 1:35, 'That holy thing that shall be born shall be the Son of God,' the Holy Spirit has given birth to you and you are the holy ones of God.

You are that separated thing that belongs absolutely to the Father. You are now his very child.[82]

It is crucial that we constantly emphasize our new identity in Christ. It keeps us in focus and prevents us from judging ourselves and others according to the flesh. In so doing, we begin to value ourselves and others in this new perspective. This perspective keeps from not losing sight of our redemption. In his book, *Identification*, E. W. Kenyon also wrote:

The teaching of Identification is the legal side of our Redemption. It unveils to us what God did in Christ for us, from the time He went to the Cross, until He sat down on the right hand of the Father. The vital side of Redemption is what the Holy Spirit through the Word is doing in us now.[83]

We gain a new confidence in who we are in Christ when we reflect on the teachings of redemption. Often, as believers, we face

[82] Kenyon, E. W. *What We Are in Christ*. Second Printing. Copyright ©2013 by Kenyon's Gospel Publishing Society. Publisher: Kenyon's Gospel Publishing Society, Lynwood WA. 98046-0973, pp. 4, 80

[83] Kenyon, E. W. *Identification—A Romance in Redemption*. Twenty-Sixth Printing. Copyright 2012 by Kenyon's Gospel Publishing Society. Publisher: Kenyon's Gospel Publishing Society, Lynwood WA. 98046-0973, pg. 7

challenges to what we believe, life "happens," our past may torment us, but one moment of reflection upon our redemption silences all these, and we rise with fresh courage. Knowing our Christlike identity will also sift out any voices of un-redemptive thought. We will discern immediately what is not in keeping with the truths of redemption. We stand in a new godly dignity in our Christlike identity, because we know we are made of the righteousness of God in Christ Jesus. Kenneth Copeland also wrote:

> In Ephesians 6:10–18, the Apostle Paul is describing the armor of God. One of the most important pieces of this armor is the breastplate of righteousness. A breastplate covers the vital parts of a soldier's body. Your right standing with God acts as that breastplate. It covers the vital part of a Christians identity—his ability to the authority provided for him in Jesus Christ. You need to put on your breastplate of righteousness and wear it victoriously. It will bring the force of righteousness into operation on your behalf.[84]

A revelation of our new identity in Christ and his righteousness is that which enables us to walk victoriously. The enemy would love for us to forget who are in Christ. When we lose sight of our true identity in Christ, we fall prey to teachings that are not in sync with redemptive truths. Neil T. Anderson shares the significance of understanding our identity:

> Understanding your identity in Christ is essential for living the Christian life.

---

[84] Copeland, Kenneth, *Now We Are in Christ Jesus*. Copyright 1980. Eagle Mountain International Church, Incorporated, a.k.a. Kenneth Copeland Ministries, Publisher: Kenneth Copeland Publications, Fort Worth, TX. 76192-0001 pp. 30–31

People cannot consistently behave in ways that are inconsistent with the way they perceive themselves. You don't change yourself by your perception. You change your perception of yourself by believing the truth. If you perceive yourself wrongly, you will live wrongly, because what you are believing is not true. If you think you are a no good-bum, you will probably live like a no-good bum. If, however, you see yourself as a child of God who is spiritually alive in Christ, you will begin to live accordingly. Next to a knowledge of God, a knowledge of who you are is by far the most important truth you can possess.

The major strategy of Satan is to distort the character of God and the truth of who we are. He can't change God and he can't do anything to change our identity and position in Christ. If, however, he can get us to believe a lie, we will live as though identity in Christ isn't true.[85]

As we hold fast to the truths of who we are in Christ, we begin to esteem others in the same way. As we understand the value of our redemption and see ourselves as God sees us, consequently, we begin to see others as God sees them. In his book, *The New Kind of Love*, E. W. Kenyon wrote:

We have been seeing men through Sense-dominated eyes. Now we can see them as the Father see them... We must close our natural Sense-ruled eyes, and

---

[85] Anderson, Neil T. *Victory Over Darkness*. E-book Edition originally created 2013. Copyright 1990 by Regal Books (First Edition), 2000 by Neil T. Anderson (Second Edition), 2013 by Neil T. Anderson (Third Edition). Publisher: Bethany House Publishers, Bloomington, MN. 55438, Chapter 2, pg. 49

through the eyes of our heart see them as the Father sees them.[86]

In his book, *You Are God's Best*, T. L. Osborn also wrote on the effect of the new creation:

The coming of Jesus Christ and the Good News has brought to us a new and positive message, of a new creation, a new birth, a new life, a new nature, a new way. 'If you are in Christ, you are a new creature: old things are passed away; behold, all things are become new (2 Cor. 5:17). The new birth is a miracle. When you come to Christ, you are made new. You are changed. Believe in that change.

Think about that change. Confess it. Sing about it. Act like you have been changed. When you stop condemning yourself, then you can stop condemning others. As you start believing in yourself, then you can believe in others.[87]

By rediscovering who we are in Christ, we also redefine ourselves as we begin the process in renewing our minds to the truths of redemption. Naturally, we become transformed into the image of Christ, to our original identity (Gen. 1:26). It is important that we learn to cooperate with this grace of the Holy Spirit's work in our lives. Oswald Chambers wrote:

Man is to be again in the image of God not by evolution, but by redemption. The meaning of

---

[86] Kenyon, E. W. *The New Kind of Love*. Twenty-First Printing. Copyright 2000 by Kenyon's Gospel Publishing Society. Publisher: Kenyon's Gospel Publishing Society, Lynwood WA. 98046-0973, pg. 33

[87] Osborn, T. L. *You Are God's Best*. Copyright 2013 by LaDonna C. Osborn. Publishers: Osborn Ministries International, Tulsa, OK. 74102, pg.31

redemption is not simply the regeneration of individuals, but that the whole human race is rehabilitated, put back to where God designed it be; consequently, any member of the human race can have the heredity of the Son of God put in him, namely, the Holy Spirit, by right of what Jesus did on the Cross.[88]

This transformation becomes tangible in our lives, and people will begin to see the embodiment of Christ's life in and through us "that ye should shew forth the praise of him who called us out of darkness into his marvelous light" (2 Peter 2:9b, KJV). When we begin to grasp our new creation identity in Christ, we learn to identify our lives with this new reality. This is our new covering, our spiritual clothing that was restored to us at the redemption Christ brought to us. Paul exhorts:

That you put on the new man which was created according to God, in true righteousness and holiness. (Ephesians 4:24, NKJV)

And have put on the new man who is renewed in knowledge according to the image of him who created him. (Colossians 3:10, NKJV)

With dignity, we can walk in the revelation of who we are in Christ and exemplify this reality to those who are yet to discover this wonderful truth. When we embrace the new realities of our redeemed identity in Christ, we no longer sense the need to depend

---

[88] Chambers, Oswald. *Conformed to His Image—The Servant as His Lord, Lessons on Living Like Jesus.* Copyright ©1995 Oswald Chambers Publications Association Limited. Publisher: Discovery House Publishers, Grand Rapids, MI. 49501, pg. 18

upon what we are in the natural for significance and authorization to minister in regions we are not native to. Instead, we can remain confident because of who we are in Christ.

10

Restored Equality

God is faithful, by whom you were called into
the fellowship of Jesus Christ our Lord.

—1 Cor. 1:9

We have discussed the importance of being born again, our redeemed status, what it means to be included in the new covenant, our privilege to pray, and what our proper spiritual clothing means to us as believers in Christ—our Christlike identity. We have defined biblical spiritual authority and how it applies in light of our righteousness in Christ, that Satan is defeated, and we are victorious in Christ's triumph. We have also discussed that through Christ's redeeming work, our true identity has been restored to us by faith in Christ. As believers in Christ, we are made into a new creation, and by this, we can confidently minister the Gospel in his name.

The effect that the "spiritual jurisdiction view" has brought was an imbalance of the believers' opportunity for Christian ministry. This also resulted in bringing about limitations and exclusion, including further inequality and comparison. This creates a gap in relationships and hinders the ability for believers to cooperate in the mandate of heaven. To cure this problem, we must shed light on the wonderful truths of redemption regarding the restored equality that it brings among Christ's redeemed community.

Since we can learn to become conscious that our original identity has been restored to us, we can identify with other believers through our restored relationship with the Father and with one another through Christ.

This was the crowning achievement in the plan of redemption, that we would not only be forgiven of our sins but also delivered from Satan's rule, that we would be born again as new creations, receiving his righteousness, brought into relationship with our heavenly Father.

Relationship—fellowship with God is what the human heart craves, yet it is also the yearning of the Father's heart. Paul indicates this aspect of restored relationship seen in the ministry of reconciliation:

> Now all things are of God who has reconciled us to Himself through Jesus Christ and has given us the ministry of reconciliation that is, that God was in Christ reconciling the world to Himself, not imputing their trespasses to them and has committed to the word of reconciliation. (2 Corinthians 5:18–19, NKJV)

We can gather the Father's intention for Christian ministry was that all who believe will be restored into fellowship with him. His intention was not just to make us his servants but that we would come into relationship with him, and Christ made this possible. Walking in this restored relationship animates our newfound identity in Christ. In her book, *God's Big Picture*, Dr. LaDonna Osborn wrote:

> The separation between the Creator and his creation that had left people isolated from God, and that had deeply fractured the human family could finally be replaced by relationship. People were not created to endure the injustice and cruelty of inequity. Human persons were never intended

to be categorized according to gender, skin color, social and academic level, or any other societal distinctive. They were created to be in a beautiful and intimate relationship with their Heavenly Father, and to enjoy unbroken fellowship and oneness with each other. Everything that God determines for his children flows out of the relationship that they have with him. The beautiful garden of relationship with God is recreated in the hearts of those who believe in Jesus Christ. God's paradise of love is restored.[89]

As believers, we can choose to believe these truths and begin to walk in the reality of our restored relationship/fellowship with our heavenly Father. This generates reconciliation with each other. We are all one in Christ, and because he dwells within each of us, we are brought into unity through the fellowship of his Son. Equality is established in our relationships with one another in his name. Therein is the magnitude of our redemption through the precious blood of Christ. We begin to identify with one another as sons and daughters of God.

Understanding the core of our identity in Christ through our restored relationship with him causes us to begin to appreciate one another in the commonality we have in this light. We identify with each other through Christ's work and no longer conform to the attitudes or prejudices of this world. We can realize reconciliation with one another based on the victory of the cross. Paul wrote to the Ephesian believers, highlighting this reconciliation and fellowship to which we have been brought together through Christ:

So then, remember that at one time you were Gentiles in the flesh—called "the uncircumcised"

[89] Osborn, LaDonna C. *God's Big Picture—Finding Yourself in God's Plan.* Copyright 2001 by LaDonna C. Osborn. Publishers: Osborn Publishers, Tulsa, OK. 74102, pp. 91–92

by those called "the circumcised," which is done in the flesh by human hands. At that time, you were without the Messiah, excluded from the citizenship of Israel, and foreigners to the covenants of the promise, without hope and without God in the world.

But now in Christ Jesus, you who were far away have been brought near by the blood of the Messiah. For He is our peace, who made both groups one and tore down the dividing wall of hostility. In his flesh, He made of no effect the law consisting of commands and expressed in regulations, so that He might create in Himself one new man from the two, resulting in peace.

He did this so that He might reconcile both to God in one body through the cross and put the hostility to death by it. When the Messiah came, He proclaimed the good news of peace to you who were far away and peace to those who were near. For through him we both have access by one Spirit to the Father.

So, then you are no longer foreigners and strangers, but fellow citizens with the saints, and members of God's household, built on the foundation of the apostles and prophets, with Christ Jesus Himself as the cornerstone. The whole building, being put together by him, grows into a holy sanctuary in the Lord. You also are being built together for God's dwelling in the Spirit. (Ephesians 2:11–22, HCSB)

"Fellow citizens" indicates our common spiritual new creation identity in the new birth by faith in Christ. The dividing wall of hostility, or as the King James Version calls it, the "middle wall," speaks of a two-fold wall at the temple in Jerusalem. First, a literal wall at the temple parted Jew and Gentile, including male and female. This wall was a stone wall which separated the court of the Gentiles from the holy place.

No Gentile or female was granted access to the other side of this wall as death was the consequence for trespassing. Yet, there was another wall of partition in the temple which separated even the common male Jew from the room called the holy of holies within the temple. Only the high priest of the temple was granted access once a year into this place and not without blood from the atoning sacrifice.

This wall signified to the Jew (male and female) that sin separated them from God, and for the Gentile, their wall signified that they were not of the circumcision, a people without a covenant with God. Even certain Gentiles of this era who were God-fearing, known as proselytes, were not allowed past the dividing wall. However, they and the Jewish women were allowed a limited nearness at the temple; thus, the court of the Gentiles and the court of the women.

Paul brings to light that this two-fold wall of partition (for both Jew and Gentile, including females) was done away with at the sacrifice of Jesus when his blood was poured out at Calvary. For the Jew (male and female), access had been granted to all of God's people into his holy presence because of Christ's blood. Yet, this access was not limited to the Jewish worshipper alone, for the sacrifice of Christ opened the way for all nations, regardless of their status, gender, or race—those who seek reconciliation with God.

We need to understand the shift that needed to take place within the mind of the Jewish believer. Most of the Jews were hostile toward the Gentiles. For even the term *Gentile* was the Jewish description in that they are a people far off from God and cut off from his chosen people.[90] In these times of the first-century church, reconciliation between Jew and Gentile, male and female, in regard to mingling and worshipping together was a radical idea. Yet, this was the intent of the Father's heart for all people. He dealt with the separation or rather segregation problem.

---

[90] Jameison, Faussett, and Brown Commentary. Ephesians 2:11–13. Copyright 1998–2017. Olive Tree Bible Software

While both groups began to multiply as followers of Christ, the apostles of Acts faced the challenge to resolve racial division between Jew and Gentile. Acts chapters ten and eleven records how God began to confront their mindset toward non-Jewish people. Divine intervention commenced in the supernatural vision which Peter experienced as this began to reshape his thinking.

Upon experiencing the outpouring of the Holy Spirit in the home of a Gentile, Cornelius, while Peter preached salvation to them, had become a definite sign that in the mind of God, Gentiles were no longer considered excluded. After this transition, Paul and Barnabas were appointed by the apostles and sent out by a witness of the Holy Spirit to evangelize the Gentile world.

The Ephesian church consisting mainly of Gentile believers was established by Paul. He writes to these believers to remind them that they are no longer strangers and foreigners but are considered fellow citizens of the household of God with Jewish believers. In other words, segregation is not a component of the Christian faith, and therefore, they have equality with all of God's people. By this reconciliation, equal opportunity grants entitlement for all believers to continue the work of Christ's ministry. This task is not limited by a person's distinguished race, tribe, or gender. Instead, in Christ, we are co-laborers together.

In another place, Paul wrote the Philippian believers (another church which he established):

> And now I want to plead with those two dear women, Euodias and Syntyche. Please, please, with the Lord's help, quarrel no more—be friends again. And I ask you, my true teammate, to help these women, for they worked side by side with me in telling the Good News to others; and they worked with Clement, too, and the rest of my fellow workers whose names are written in the Book of Life. (Philippians 4:2–3, TLB)

Firstly, this passage of scripture indicates two women who were co-laborers with Paul and had been at odds with each other. He urges them to put aside their differences and that they seek reconciliation for the sake of the Gospel and Christian unity. He does not start his letter to this church by directly centering in on them but first teaches about the humility of Christ (Philippians 2) and discreetly addresses these two women to be like-minded. His concern for them was the disunity that began to occur among them. His pastoral heart responded to help them deal with their conflict in a godly manner.[91]

Another part which comes to light in this reference is within the fact that these two women labored in the Gospel with Paul; it is instructive to us today. It was his deliverance from prejudice toward women. Jewish men did not associate with women, especially in public. In Jewish culture, women did not have equality with men, even in the old covenant.

Paul walked in the revelation of the new creation reality. If he did not have this understanding, women would not be seen to be working alongside with him in the ministry. Had he not been delivered from his own prejudice, he would not have partnered with non-Jewish believers as equal co-laborers. The Lord used Paul to go against the stream of discriminative mindsets of his day. His radical conversion into Christianity illuminated his perception of others through the scope of redemption. This is revealed throughout his ministry and the numerous epistles he wrote. That the "whosever believeth" meant just that.

This Gospel of salvation was and is meant for all who believe, that all who believe are given equal opportunity in the Christian faith, and that segregation of race, tribe, gender, status, or wealth is done away with. When our minds have been renewed and when we have been delivered from prejudiced mindsets, we are liberated by the compassion of the Father's heart to go into all the world, proclaiming the good news. With the right perspective, we no longer singularize or limit others in their call to reach the nations with the love of Jesus.

[91] *Expositor's Bible Commentary*. Philippians 4:2 (13 vol. series). Copyright 1998–2017. Olive Tree Bible Software

11

Laboring in the Lord's Harvest— Crossing Cultural Dynamics

We are privileged to represent Christ in this world and to go forth with confidence in his name. So far, we have discussed the truths of being born again—that in Christ, we are made new creations. We have examined that being made a new creation also means that we have received his righteous nature. We have determined that being born again also covers that all believers have been included in the new covenant. We studied the core of our restored identity in Christ.

We have also observed the position of righteousness as the base of our spiritual authority in Christ. From this position, we have equality with one another based upon our being in Christ through his work. By this, we have been brought into fellowship and reconciliation with one another enabling us to be co-laborers in the work of the ministry. We will now look into the dynamics considering our communication of the Gospel message in matters pertaining to cultural barriers. All believers are called to share in the ministry of the Gospel, no matter their culture.

The Lord of the Harvest

After these things the Lord appointed seventy others also and sent them two by two before his face into every city and place where He Himself was about to go. Then He said to them, "The harvest truly is great, but the laborers are few; therefore, pray the Lord of the harvest to send out laborers into his harvest. (Luke 10:1–2, NKJV)

The commissioning of Jesus in Luke chapter ten presents principles to which we can apply as we walk in our spiritual authority. First of all, we see that "the Lord appointed...and sent them" (Luke 10:1). The concept of being sent by the Lord himself in and of itself is the force which backs up our ability to walking in spiritual authority. If he is not doing the sending, then there is no empowerment available to us in matters of doing the works of the kingdom.

Kingdom power is backed by heaven's sending. This power or authority cannot be given by man or transferred from any person in order to minister healing and deliverance in his name to the one in need. As we have established earlier, Jesus straightforwardly stated that all authority had been given to him in heaven and on earth. Ability to operate in this authority comes through the sending of the Lord of the harvest. As we are in obedience to his sending, we have the means to minister in his name.

Secondly, Jesus speaks of the harvest as being truly great, yet we are reminded that this harvest is his harvest. Knowing who the Lord of the harvest is should command a respect within us as to who we answer to. No man on earth can grant us authority to do kingdom works in the regions to which we intend to minister. Neither can any person "transfer supernaturally" this spiritual authority. Transference of spiritual authority is given by the Lord Jesus.

We must consider that if the Lord of the harvest is the One who is sending us, we do not need to wait for man's approval in order to carry out the mandate with which we are sent. The author states this in light of the misconception about "spiritual gatekeepers" in certain regions who also believe they are positioned to welcome and grant their approval before any foreigner can minister in their area. This view has brought confusion in Christian ministry, and as well, it has brought much hindrance to the progressive work of the Gospel.

We see in context of Luke chapter ten that Jesus did not indicate that our being sent was restricted to racial, tribal, or gender factors in order to have sanction to minister. However, we do see that he was concerned for the souls of mankind no matter their natural birth. Our source of power and authority to preaching the Gospel of the kingdom and as well as doing the works of the kingdom has been authorized in our being sent by the Lord of the harvest.

In matters of being welcomed, Jesus instructs his disciples:

> But whatever house you enter, first say, "Peace to this house." And if a son of peace is there, your peace will rest on it; if not, it will return to you… Whatever city you enter, and they receive you, eat such things as are set before you…But whatever city you enter, and they do not receive you, go out into its streets and say, The very dust of your city which clings to us we wipe off against you. Nevertheless, know this, that the kingdom of God has come near you (Luke 10:5–6,8–12, NKJV).

These instructions speak of our relational conduct among the people we are sent to while being conscious of who we are representing—the Lord himself. In this passage of scripture, Jesus teaches how we as his ministers ought to handle being rejected. These instructions have no implications about any "spiritual gatekeeper" who should grant permission to exercise spiritual authority to minister. If we are not received, we are instructed to wipe the dust off our feet as a testimony against those who refused the Gospel. Therefore, the product of our spiritual authority stems from being sent, and those who do not receive us simply will not benefit from the blessing of which the Lord intended.

In Matthew 5:11–12 and Luke 6:22–23, Jesus places further emphasis on how to handle being reviled and/or persecuted in that we are to rejoice and know that we are blessed. His instructions in Luke chapter ten are in sync with these attitudes. We are challenged not to act like victims but how to behave wisely and while not losing our confidence in our heavenly mandate.

K. P. Yohannan in his book, *Against the Wind*, wrote:

> Dependence on the Lord alone is central to our lives as we live for and serve God. Our attitude must always reflect the belief that God is our only source—not information, evaluation and judgements from culture, someone else's views or our own prejudices.[92]

The principle of dependence on the Lord alone is an emphasis that must be brought to light in a fresh new way. Walking in this reality, we keep ourselves from taking any credit to ourselves. What then does Paul's statement, "Christ in you the hope of glory" (Colossians 1:27, NKJV), truly mean? How does this apply to the believer? What does this have to do with our biological identity in matters of confidently walking in our spiritual authority? How is this related to us as we are ministering the Gospel? We are exhorted in Philippians 2:13, "We are the circumcision, who worship God in the Spirit, rejoice in Christ Jesus and have no confidence in the flesh" (NKJV). Watchman Nee wrote:

> In the work of God today, things are often so constituted upon all such work is uncompromising: 'Apart from me ye can do nothing' (John 15:5). Such work as man can do apart from God is wood, hay, stubble—and the test of fire will

[92] Yohannon, K. P. *Against the Wind—Finishing Well in a World of Compromise.* Copyright 2004. Publisher: GFA Books, a Division of Gospel for Asia, 1800 Golden Trail Court, Carrollton, TX. 75010, pg. 87

prove it so. For divine work can only be done with divine power, and that power is to be found in the Lord Jesus alone. It is made available to us in him on the resurrection side of the cross.[93]

As believers, we are challenged to keep an attitude of humility while depending upon and remaining confident in the One who dwells within us. We must never allow a superiority complex to inhabit our way of relating with those different than ourselves. Paul addresses this kind of attitude as he reflects himself to exemplify the aspect of humility:

[t]hough I also might have confidence in the flesh. If anyone else thinks he may have confidence in the flesh, I more so: circumcised the eighth day, of the stock of Israel, of the tribe of Benjamin, a Hebrew of the Hebrews; concerning the law, a Pharisee; concerning zeal, persecuting the church; concerning the righteousness which is in the law, blameless. But what things were gain to me, these I have counted loss for Christ. Yet indeed I also count all things loss for the excellence of the knowledge of Christ Jesus my Lord, for whom I have suffered the loss of all things, and count them as rubbish, that I may gain Christ and be found in him, not having my own righteousness, which is from the law, but that which is through faith in Christ, the righteousness which is from God by faith; that I may know him and the power of his resurrection, and the fellowship of his sufferings, being conformed to his death, if, by any means, I may attain to the

---

[93] Nee, Watchman. *Sit, Walk, Stand—The Process of Christian Maturity*. Copyright 2009 by CLC Ministries International. Publishers: CLC Publications, Fort Washington, PA. 19034, pg. 61

resurrection from the dead. (Philippians 3:4–11, NKJV)

As we have stated earlier, Paul dealt with two women among the Philippian believers who had a certain conflict with each other. Before he confronts them, he draws their attention to the humility that we as believers—as partners in ministry—ought to walk in. By using himself as an example that as a male Jew, raised in Judaism, having gained the title of Pharisee who obeyed the law of God without fault that this did not gain him confidence as a believer in Christ. This clues us in to the possible dynamics which these believers were dealing with. Self-confidence only breeds contempt and moves us away from Christ-centered confidence.

Near the close of his letter to the Philippians, Paul writes, "I can do all things through Christ who strengthens me" (Vs. 4:13, NKJV). We can apply this truth: Our source of confidence is Christ within us.

The prize to our Christian walk is not centered on our accomplishments or what we are in the flesh, but rather, it is upon knowing Christ and seeing his power and glory come forth through our lives. We ought to believe in one another and appreciate Christ within each other.

We cannot get the work of the ministry done if we do not value one another in our agreement with the message of the Gospel.

There Were Certain Greeks

The Gospel of John follows the trail of events leading up to the triumphal entry of Christ at the entrance of Jerusalem. In chapter twelve, we find that the multitude which arrived at Jerusalem were there in response to an incredible miracle at the raising of Lazarus who had been dead for four days. There were many who bore witness of this resurrection. As a result, these same witnesses spread the word, resulting in many responding to go to where Jesus was about to appear. The significance of this miracle was that this was medically impossible for it to happen. The fact that Jesus had done it signified to them the inevitable—he was their Messiah.

Therefore, as they heard of his coming to Jerusalem for the Passover, they waited at the entrance of the city to welcome him with praise (see John 11:12–18).

At this entry, certain Greeks also responded and approached one of his disciples, Philip, by requesting to see Jesus personally. We see these Greek fellows used the protocol of the time, keeping in mind that Jews did not associate with Gentiles. Thus, approaching Philip instead of Jesus directly.

Jesus's response to Philip was quite intriguing. "And if I am lifted up from the earth, will draw all peoples to Myself" (vs. 32, NKJV). This scripture reference has often been read to emphasize an important principle in Christian ministry—lift up Jesus. That in itself is a crucial conviction to live by. However, in order to understand his response, verse 32 must be read in context with the previous words from verses 22–32. Let's read them through:

> [t]he hour has come that the Son of Man should be glorified. Most assuredly, I say to you, unless a grain of wheat falls into the ground and dies, it remains alone; but if it dies, it produces much grain. He who loves his life will lost it, and he who hates his life in this world will keep it for eternal life. If anyone serve Me, let him follow me; and where I am there My servant will be also If anyone serve Me, him My Father will honor. Now my soul is troubled and what shall I say? Father, save Me from this hour? But for this purpose I came to this hour. Father glorify your name. Then a voice came from heaven, saying, I have both glorified it and will glorify it again. Therefore, the people who stood by and heard it said that it had thundered. Others said, An angel has spoken to him. Jesus answered and said, this voice did not come because of Me, but for your sake. Now is the judgement of this world: now the ruler of this world will be cast out. And if I

am lifted up from the earth, will draw all peoples
to Myself. (John 11:22–32, NKJV)

Why did the Greeks come? They heard of the phenomenal miracle of Lazarus being raised from the dead. Why did Jesus respond
the way he did to Philip and Andrew's request for the Greeks to
see him personally? This was intended to prepare his disciples what
they must understand: that all nations (including the Greeks) will
have the privilege to come to him. His heart's desire was not only
for their Native people—the Jewish nation—being subject to receive
salvation but that all people would be saved. That when he was lifted
up—on the cross—his ministry would not end there.

The time would come when they, as his followers, would continue his work and that this work would not be for one select group.
As his disciples, they were to also include in their ministry an outreach to the Gentile world with the message of salvation. He indicated an all-inclusive involvement among all nationalities for the
greater work of the Gospel.

Jesus Forbids Sectarianism

John said to him, "Teacher, we saw a man
who does not follow along with us driving out
demons in Your name, and we forbade him to do
it, because he is not one of our band [of Your dis-
ciples]." But Jesus said, "Do not restrain or hin-
der or forbid him; for no one who does a mighty
work in My name will soon afterward be able to
speak evil of Me." For he who is not against us is
for us. (Mark 9:38–40, AMPC).

John spoke up, "Master, we saw a man using
your name to expel demons and we stopped
him because he wasn't of our group." Jesus said,
"Don't stop him. If he's not an enemy, he's an
ally." (Luke 9:49–50, The Message Translation)

Both Mark and Luke related the same conversation that was held between Jesus and his disciples as both accounts exposed a sectarianist mindset which Jesus forbade among his disciples. By the disciples expressing "he is not one of our band" or "he is not one of our group," it uncovered the frame of mind which his disciples held. Jesus corrected their thinking.

This revealed their need to have their minds renewed in this area, and Jesus enabled them to see clearly. *Expositors Bible Commentary* sheds light on Jesus's response:

> This verse is proverbial in form. The man was not against Jesus. Apparently, he had not yet joined the group of Jesus's disciples. Perhaps he represents those who are "on the way" to joining the body of believers and who should be welcomed rather than repulsed. In a different situation (Mt 12:30), Jesus used a reverse form of this proverb and did so without contradicting the truth set forth here in Luke.[94]

Sectarianism becomes fostered by those who hold the erroneous "spiritual jurisdiction view" that those who are not of a certain region, race, or gender as they believe that these are unauthorized to minister the Gospel in their area. This discriminative attitude breeds segregation.

Sectarianism defined: denoting or concerning a sect or sects: of an action carried out on the grounds of membership of a sect, denomination, or other group: rigidly following the doctrines of a sect or other group.[95]

---

[94] *Expositor's Bible Commentary.* Luke 9:50 (13 vol. series). Copyright 1998–2017. Olive Tree Bible Software

[95] *Oxford Dictionary of English.* Third Edition. Copyright 1998, 2003, 2005, 2010 by Oxford University Press. Publisher: Oxford University Press, Great Clarendon Street, Oxford, oX2 6DP, Oxford, New York, pg. 1609

We can conclude that the following three terms—sectarianism, racism, and discrimination—are intertwined symptoms of human pride propagating a superiority complex breeding segregation and separation. These do not reflect the values of true Christian faith.

In dealing with these issues of sectarianism, racism, and discrimination, we must seek reconciliation within ourselves and seek to reach out with love and compassion to those we have viewed wrongly. Knowing that we are working for the same Lord means we are on the same team. This common effort is meant for the advancement of the kingdom of God as we focus on him who is the author of our salvation. This Christlike attitude produces a change of heart by simply letting go of unredeemed thinking. In his book, *The Reconstruction of the Church*, E. Stanley Jones wrote:

> This verse is decisive: 'He that gathers not with me scatters.' If this means anything it means that if we gather around Jesus, if 'Jesus is Lord,' we can transcend all our other differences and find unity in a common Lord; but if we don't do that, if we gather around something else, however good, we scatter. Christ-centric we gather; any-thing-else-centric, we scatter.[96]

It is crucial that our gathering is centered on Christ by allowing his heart to transform our hearts and lives for the greater work of the Gospel. The work of the ministry is not about us.

Focusing on the truths of redemption causes us to see past our differences, and we see the bigger picture when we begin to understand true biblical equality.

---

[96] Jones, E. Stanley. *The Reconstruction of the Church—On What Pattern?* Copyright 1970 by Abingdon Press. Publisher: Abingdon Press, Nashville, TN. pg. 93

Welcoming the One Sent

Matthew chapter ten records how Jesus gave instructions to his disciples before he sent them out to minister in his name. He taught about a reward that would be released to those who received them:

> Anyone who welcomes you welcomes me, and anyone who welcomes me welcomes the one who sent me. Whoever welcomes a prophet as a prophet will receive a prophet's reward, and whoever welcomes a righteous person as a righteous person will receive a righteous person's reward. And if anyone gives even a cup of cold water to one of these little ones who is my disciple, truly I tell you, that person will certainly not lose their reward. (Matthew 10:40–42, NIV)

We learn from this teaching given by the Lord the concept of being welcomed and a reward that follows. Jesus knew that his disciples were likely to be rejected in some places; however, the focus of the lesson was not merely in being rejected. Rather, it was in their being received. Those who received them were receiving him whom they represented. In being received, they can expect the divine reward to be released to that group of people; the ministry of Christ would manifest.

We see this principle realized in Matthew's account on one occasion during Jesus's ministry at Nazareth. "He did not do mighty works there because of their unbelief" (Matthew 13:58a, NKJV). First of all, the people of Nazareth did not receive Jesus, even though this was his native town. The divine blessing—the reward—was not released in this town because they did not receive him. Had they believed him, many would have been blessed with their needs met. We see that even Christ could not perform miracles in his hometown based on the fact that they did not believe or receive him. They judged him in the natural by saying they knew his family. This familiarity of the natural seemed to breed contempt and hindered them from perceiving the gift of God among them.

This opens our eyes to the wrong assumption that one has extra spiritual authority in the place of their natural birth origin. If this "spiritual jurisdiction view" is of truth, we must ask: Why then could not Jesus perform miracles in his home community, even though they did not believe him? He should have had the ability to operate in spiritual authority since this would have been his spiritual jurisdiction. However, the scriptures tell us that the reason he could not perform miracles was due to their unbelief.

Luke 9:51–53 shows another place where he was rejected by the Samaritans. The issue at hand had nothing to do with the natural birthright to where a servant of the Lord is from. His ability to minister was conditional to their believing in him if they received him.

The flip side of the coin has to do with our obedience to the Lord in being sent.

Obviously, as we read throughout the four Gospels, we discover that of the many places to which Jesus was sent, those that did receive and believe his Word, the reward he was sent with was imparted. That reward is the manifested anointing which brought numerous healings, and many miracles were performed. Mark 16:16, "And these signs will follow those that believe: in My name they will" (NKJV). These signs will follow "those that believe." We are given authority in his name by which we will continue the work of his ministry. Spiritual authority is not based in our own name or natural birth identity in order that we will be able to minister the Gospel to the regions that we, as his ministers, are sent.

What we glean from these words of Jesus, "whoever welcomes you, welcomes me," ought to bring us to the understanding that as we receive (welcome) those whom he sends, we are receiving him based on our faith in him. The other aspect to this truth is that those who we are sent to will receive us based on their faith in Christ. Dependability to minister should not be based in our biological factors in order to be received as a minister of the Lord. Jesus exemplified this for us. They received him because they had faith in the One who sent him.

They received him not because of his natural birth origin. The result of those who received him were blessed with healing. Those who rejected him were those who had been judging him by the natural senses, perhaps envious of his wide reception by the people. Those who judged him and rejected him based on the natural were those who did not receive the divine blessing that he came with.

It is common that the desire of all missionaries is to be received by the people to which they are sent. There is the awareness of the need to understand the culture, world views, religious beliefs, and history of the people they intend to reach. Too often, more time is spent becoming familiarized with the people that the message and the ministry intended becomes jaded as they search for relevancy with the people. Though sincere in seeking bridges in order to earn a voice among the people, the sent missionary becomes an advocate for the culture and is disillusioned with their mandate. These dynamics have also fostered the mistaken position on the "spiritual jurisdiction view."

It appears wise to be received based on the natural birth identity since this also appeals to the natural senses as they seek to avoid rejection. The writer ponders perhaps if we had confidence in the biblical mandate we have been given from heaven, including the message of the Gospel, we would not allow ourselves to be pressured into compromising the scriptures. We do not need to reinterpret the message in order to have rid ourselves of all discriminative thinking. In fact, the Gospel message changes our own prejudices toward any who are different than ourselves. Sharing Christ's love without compromising his message is powerful and effective when done with the right motives. The Gospel inspires us to reach across cultural barriers to help many become reconciled to God without changing the fundamentals of Christian truth.

12

The Gospel of Peace

When we read the earlier part of Luke chapter nine where Jesus sent out his disciples to do the works which he showed them, he included instructions about how our conduct should be when we are received and when we are not received. This conversation is also recorded in Matthew 10:5–14 and Mark 6:10–11. The principle of seeking the place of peace or the "person of peace" among those who would receive your ministry is often highlighted.

However, as we look carefully into this passage regarding the stance taken with the "spiritual jurisdiction view," we find that this scripture reference is not in sync with the implied notion about seeking the permission of a "gatekeeper." Rather, it is about the principle of a peaceable gospel. We can observe that Jesus did not prerequisite the permission of a "gatekeeper" in order to begin sharing the Gospel in the acclaimed "gatekeeper's" native land.

Most often, when you have been received by the local people, including those influential ones, naturally there is peace. The objective we seek is about building relationships with these local people in a peaceable way without compromising your message or your mandate.

However, if your ministry has been rejected, you are not obligated to assert your ministry by coercion. Jesus instructed the disciples to "shake the dust off your feet." In other words, "Move on." The followers of Jesus did this very thing as we read in Acts 13:51 where

THE BIRTH THAT COUNTS

they came into conflict with unbelievers at Antioch; they literally shook the dust off their feet. The emphasis about the Lord's instruction involves how to handle yourself when faced with conflict when your ministry is not received. We need an attitude of humility.

In other words, we do not need to insist our right to minister the Gospel. The true attitude of the Gospel is contrary to colonialist mindsets as though we intend to "take over." The Gospel message proposes to be a peaceful message of good news. It is the Gospel of Peace. As often has been stated, "People don't care about how much you know, until they know how much you care." Consider these few organizations that not only enter a community with a Bible in one hand but also with their shirt sleeves folded up on their arms and ready to lend a helpful hand who in the writers' opinion exemplify a non-threatening approach in advocating the Gospel of Peace:

> The Mennonite Central Committee of Canada have a practical ministry of helps as a means to sharing the Gospel to a hurting world by responding to basic human needs as they work for peace and justice in places traumatized by war or natural disasters.[97]

The Samaritan's Purse is another organization that practices similar deeds in order to reach a community with the love of Jesus. The following is an excerpt from their own mission's statement:

> Samaritan's Purse is a nondenominational evangelical Christian organization providing spiritual and physical aid to hurting people around the world. Since 1970, Samaritan's Purse has helped meet needs of people who are victims of war, poverty, natural disasters, disease, and famine with the purpose of sharing God's love through

---

[97] https://mcccanada.ca/learn/about/mission

his Son, Jesus Christ. The organization serves the Church worldwide to promote the Gospel of the Lord Jesus Christ.[98]

Not only is this seen in the Samaritan's Purse mission statement as portrayed in their numerous works, their volunteers practice these basic principles all over the world regardless of culture. Although we can spend much time examining numerous ministries who also focus on help and service among communities in need, the writer wants to highlight one more example: A personal experience related by a missionary participating with a particular ministry whose focus was to hold Gospel Tent Meetings. This description helps one to broaden their thinking in matters of flexibility and grace while still being able to carry out one's "Gospel-mission work (names of community and individuals will remain disclosed):"

> The Gospel Tent Team arrived at a certain First Nations reservation on a clear sunny day when they were scheduled to begin setting up their Gospel Tent. This northern community and area were surrounded by forest fires. That day, the team was evacuated along with the community to a nearby town. Since the Gospel Tent team had their own accommodations, they were able to set up their RV trailers in the campground of the same town that the people had been sent to. Upon hearing what location which the people were being sent for their meals while they waited for evacuation orders to be lifted, the team approached the Chief of the hosting First Nations Reservation for the evacuees, "What could we do to help?" He suggested that the team should volunteer in the kitchen to help serve the

---

[98] https://www.samritanspurse.org/our-ministry/about-us

meals for the evacuees of which the team was eager to do. Three meals a day, the team volunteered to assist the head cook and serve the meals to the evacuees. Since this was a stressful time, the head cook asked if any team members could sing Gospel songs to help the people have peace while they ate their meals. Two teams were then dispersed. One to serve in the kitchen, the other was appointed to sing Gospel songs. After the third day, the people began to ask the team to set up their Gospel Tent in the grass next to the building. The people went to their Chief requesting if the team could be allowed to set up the Gospel Tent and hold evening services.

After permission was granted, the Gospel Tent was set up and the evening services commenced.

The result of this effort: The head cook, including her husband of whom both were suspicious of Christians, gave their hearts to Jesus as they saw the team work along with her in the kitchen and the team also would not accept payment for their volunteer services. Others among the evacuees along with those living in the hosting reserve also received ministry.

The Gospel Tent Team realized, had they left the area and canceled their time there, they would have missed an opportunity to show the love of Jesus. This turn of events became a strengthening of their reception of the Gospel Tent Team among the people including their relationship with them as the Gospel Tent Team continues to return to this community.[99]

---

[99] Interview held by Author White, September 13, 2018, Date of shared experience occurred: July, 2012. Interviewees name withheld by agreement.

Perhaps these various kinds of practical ways ought to be reflected as one considers how a ministry can exemplify the Gospel message of peace. Instead of pursuing "traditional" and "ceremonial" accoutrements in order to be "culturally relevant," the writer will suggest a simple act of love shown by good works will open the door to any heart, no matter what kind of inhibitions people may have toward Christians. Even so, if we experience that we will not be accepted in spite of our good intentions and good works, we can know that there are many other places that need our message of good news. It is the art of entering with peace and leaving peaceably.

Let us read again the words of Jesus from Luke 9:4–5:

> Whatever house you enter, stay there, and from there depart. And whoever will not receive you, when you go out of that city, shake off the very dust from your feet as a testimony against them.

"Whatever house you enter" indicates a non-restriction regardless of nationality or any such matter. This simply has to do with the person who welcomes you into their home, in their reception of the Gospel message that you have already begun to share. The next train of thought is "whoever will not receive you, when you go out of that city, shake the very dust from your feet as a testimony against them." In other words, do not make an issue of being rejected while you're there and after when you leave. Leave it to God to judge them. *Expositor's Revised Commentary* gives these insights to Luke 9:4–5:

> The disciples should receive hospitality graciously. Hospitality was important as well as necessary in days of difficult traveling conditions and poor accommodations at inns. The disciples are not to move about from house to house, a practice that might gain them more support but would insult their hosts.
>
> The disciples will also encounter those who refuse them a welcome. As a solemn sym-

bol of judgment, the disciples are to "shake the dust" of an unresponsive town off of their feet, just as Jewish travelers might do on returning from pagan territory (Str-B 1:571). This action expressed symbolically what Jesus would say about Korazin and Bethsaida in 10:13–15. Jesus himself later wept over Jerusalem's unresponsiveness (19:41).

Elsewhere Jesus specifies the kind of person who is to have the privilege of supporting the disciples. He must be a "worthy [axios, GK 545] person" (Mt 10:11), a "man of peace" (huios eirēnēs, lit., "son of peace," Lk 10:6). Such a person is clearly in sympathy with the message brought by Jesus's disciples.[100]

In keeping with *Expositor's* words, as we contemplate who is the "man of peace," we can identify that this person is the one who receives the message of the good news to which we are sent to proclaim, regardless of any person's national ethnicity. In contrast to the notion is this "man of peace" as being associated with a "gatekeeper" as this is a supposition of those who favor the "spiritual jurisdiction view" on their misgivings of a verse of scripture like that of Luke 9:4–5. This association becomes misdirected above the literal interpretation and application of what Jesus intended to teach. To state it bluntly, that "man of peace" is that person who has been deemed worthy, because they believed the Gospel that has already begun to be proclaimed within that person's community. Simply, their worthiness is not due to their being native to their region.

Reading the same account from Matthew 10:11–13, "And into whatsoever city or town ye shall enter, enquire who in it is worthy; and there abide till ye go thence. And when ye come into an house, salute it. And if the house be worthy, let your peace come upon it: but

---

[100] *Expositor's Bible Commentary.* Luke 9:4–5 (13 vol. series). Copyright 1998–2017. Olive Tree Bible Software

if it be not worthy, let your peace return to you" (KJV). Continuing with *Expositor's* commentary:

> To settle into the house of a "worthy" person implies that the disciples were not to shop around for the most comfortable quarters. Here "worthy" probably does not refer to a morally upright, honorable, or religious person but to one willing and able to receive an apostle of Jesus and the gospel of the kingdom.[101]

Mark 6:10, "And he said unto them, In what place soever ye enter into an house, there abide till ye depart from that place." (KJV). Again, *Expositor's* grants us more insight to the relational dynamics on this account given in Mark:

> Jesus gave the instruction here to protect the good reputation of the disciples. Whenever they accepted hospitality in a home, they were to lodge there until they left that town, even if more comfortable or attractive lodgings were offered to them. The human tendency would be gradually to move up the social ladder as friendships were developed with more influential people. Such actions would show unchristian favoritism (Jas 2:1–13), create spiritual disunity, and run contrary to the missionary's absolute dependence on God.[102]

We can now ascertain how straightforward the Lord's instructions are to his followers. In our efforts of Gospel outreach, we are

[101] *Expositor's Bible Commentary*. Matthew 10:11 (13 vol. series). Copyright 1998–2017. Olive Tree Bible Software

[102] *Expositor's Bible Commentary*. Mark 6:10 (13 vol. series). Copyright 1998–2017. Olive Tree Bible Software

taught from scripture to focus on those individuals who believe and receive the Gospel. We are to do so without partiality to a person's status, income, race, or any other preferences to a person's accoutrements. By their reception of the message, we are able to continue a Gospel work, teaching God's Word should they desire for more of what you have to teach. There is no need to over-spiritualize and insinuate any notion of seeking permission from a "gatekeeper" before you can begin to share the Gospel in their community.

Neither is there a need to wait for these acclaimed individuals to transfer their anointing or spiritual authority onto us. Instead, we see it is about the indication that once the Gospel has been received, you then have the momentum to resume teaching about Christian faith to those receptive hearts.

Again, Jesus was also clear on how we are to handle ourselves when we are not received. "And whosoever shall not receive you, nor hear you, when ye depart thence, shake off the dust under your feet for a testimony against them. Verily I say unto you, It shall be more tolerable for Sodom and Gomorrah in the day of judgment, than for that city" (Mark 6:11, KJV). One more insight from *Expositor's* as this helps to understand what Jesus was instructing his disciples:

> Jesus knew that the mission of the Twelve would not always be accepted. Had not he also been rejected by many? So he instructed them on how to act in such circumstances. The shaking of the dust from their feet may be understood in the light of the Jewish custom of removing carefully the dust from both clothes and feet before reentering Jewish territory (m. Ohalot 2:3; m. Tehar. 4:5l; b. Šabb. 15b). For the Jews, heathen dust was defiling. The significance of the act here is to declare the place to be heathen and to make it clear that those who rejected the message must now answer for themselves, as apparently meant by the phrase "as a testimony against them." The

disciples' message, like that of Jesus, brings judgment as well as salvation.[103]

If we are to appropriate these instructions of our Lord, we will
recognize that we do not need to become apologetic or try to become
"culturally appealing" and wait for a "gatekeeper's" permission before
we can begin to share the Gospel message. When we attempt to do
so, this kind of a slant often leads into compromising the message
and takes away the focus of the mission of the message. Instead, we
see that Jesus instructed his followers to simply move on and focus on
those who choose to believe what we have already begun to proclaim.
That in itself is remaining peaceable within a community.

As we are dealing with the "spiritual jurisdiction view," we
will now move on to the next aspect in matters pertaining to other
dynamics to cross-cultural ministry.

A look at cross-cultural ministry:

As we consider ministering cross-culturally, Jesus is our prime
example as we see how he ministered to the multitudes as well as to
the individuals regardless of their race or gender. In her book, *Equal
Redemption for All*, Marie Brown wrote:

> When studying the life of Jesus and examining
> his encounters with people, one discovers God's
> plan. Jesus placed no conditions or limitations on
> people because of their culture, race, sex, amount
> of education or wealth. Rather, Jesus treated all
> people as equal by looking on their hearts and
> responding to each individual at the point of his
> or her need.[104]

---

[103] *Expositor's Bible Commentary*. Mark 6:11 (13 vol. series). Copyright 1998–
2017. Olive Tree Bible Software

[104] Brown, Marie, *Equal Redemption for All*. Copyright 1990 by H. Marie Brown.
Publisher: Marie Brown Ministries, Tulsa, OK. 74170 pg. 36

What God honors is our faith in him. Jesus always emphasized the faith that people had in him. He said about the Centurion, "I have not found such great faith, not even in Israel" (Luke 7:9c, NKJV). He said to the blind man who received his sight, "Receive your sight, your faith has made you well" (Luke 18:42, NKJV). Again, to the woman with the issue of blood, he affirms, "Be of good cheer, daughter, your faith has made you well" (Matthew 9:22, NKJV). To the Gentile woman seeking healing on her daughter's behalf, he also says, "O woman, great is your faith! Let it be to you as you desire" (Matthew 15:28, NKJV).

What we learn from this is that our objective as ministers of the Gospel is to stir up faith in Jesus within the hearts of those we minister to. We must encourage people to have faith in the One who can meet their need.

This faith was not conditional to a person's natural birth but in the person of Jesus Christ.

With this in mind, as ministers or missionaries, it is important not to be ignorant of the cultures we are sent to. This evokes a question: Where do we draw the line in our relevancy with the message which we are stewards of without compromising the biblical text? We need the wisdom of God in these sensitive matters (see Appendix G).

The author cautions readers to rethink their approach to contextualization. The fundamentals of Christianity do not change with our ever-changing society. In truth, the Gospel was not meant to be faddish. Yet, in its simplicity, the message of the Gospel is powerful and effective. "The Gospel is the power of God unto salvation to everyone who believes" (Romans 1:16, NKJV). There is a working together that is needful to make Gospel outreach ministry successful. We can learn from each other in order to advance in our efforts to advocate the furtherance of the Gospel.

Let's take a moment to consider an example regarding certain cities which are built upon pilings (stilt-like structures) along the ocean shoreline of the western coast of North America. Amazingly, some of these communities have structured highways, streets, and sections throughout much of their downtown corridor which are built on these specially engineered pilings while the rest of the town is built upward alongside the mountainside. This kind of structure has been engineered to keep the community safe from the constant changes in the oceans tide levels.

These tide changes are extreme. If you have been to one of these kinds of places, you will learn quickly how far the tide goes out and how closely underneath the street the ocean waters return. Consider if these cities constantly changed its boundaries and adjusted its pilings with the tides, it would never be an established dwelling. Why? The reason is that these tides change twice a day. However, these communities are established on well-founded pilings for commuters, businesses, and residents to continue on living securely. Watching the livelihood of these streets, you will quickly notice that they are filled with all kinds of moving traffic on a twenty-four-hour basis; this gives you confidence that these pilings are secure.

This is a picture about the fundamental truths of the Gospel. They do not change with the latest trends (tides) of this world's system or ideals. Our faith is secure in the established truths of scripture, and we do not need to worry if they will hold in the future. In learning to communicate the concepts of the Gospel cross-culturally, we are challenged not to change its meaning in order to secure our ministry efforts and gain acceptance in any society we minister. In our efforts to approach contextualization, we must keep in mind these words of Paul:

> Don't copy the behavior and customs of this world but be a new and different person with a fresh newness in all you do and think. Then you will learn from your own experience how his ways will really satisfy you. (Romans 12:2, The Living Bible)

Our text—the Word of God—is the authority in all things. Although it is vital to communicate the Gospel in an understandable way in the heart language of the people to which we are sent, there are no special cases for compromise of the message in order to find relevancy. Paul used the approach of relevancy in his time at Athens as we find in Acts chapter seventeen. He uses words to which these Athenians are familiar without changing the concepts of Gospel truth. *Expositor's Commentary* gives this insight to Paul's attempt to share the Gospel at Athens.

> Paul is not suggesting by the use of such maxims that God is to be thought of in terms of the god Zeus of Greek polytheism or Stoic pantheism. Rather, he is arguing that the poets whom his hearers recognized as authorities have at least to some extent corroborated his message. In his search for a measure of common ground with his hearers, he is, so to speak, disinfecting and rebaptizing the words of two Greek poets for his own purposes. Quoting these Greek poets in support of his teaching sharpened his message for his particular audience. But despite its form, Paul's address was thoroughly biblical and Christian in its content.[105]

This approach did not result in the response as Paul had hoped. The thought of a resurrection was of no interest to the Greek philosopher, for their interpretation of life had much to do with the present life. In his attempt to speak a relevant message, he had their attention for a time, but the hearers did not relate to his message, save only a few who further inquired after his speech.[106]

As communicators of the Gospel, we do not favor these kinds of results. Paul in his wisdom knew to move on and focus on those who did desire to discuss what he attempted to explain. Interesting that there is no record of a church at Athens in these first-century times. He did not syncretize the Gospel message with their philosophical

---

[105] *Expositor's Bible Commentary*. Acts 17:28 (13 vol. series). Copyright 1998–2017. Olive Tree Bible Software

[106] *Expositor's Bible Commentary*. Acts 17:29–31 (13 vol. series). Copyright 1998–2017. Olive Tree Bible Software

ideas in order to gain acceptance of his message or ministry. He had the wisdom to know the difference, and we see this when he began to speak of Christ's resurrection.

What we learn from this example is that contextualization and relevancy doesn't always work. Many today will adjoin Jesus as another religious icon but struggle over Christ's own words, "I am the way, the truth and the life and no one comes to the Father except by me" (John 14:6, NKJV). It is difficult for them to accept that he is the only way to the Father, the only source of truth and life. Those who struggle want to continue equating world religions, culture, and tradition to their world view as they maintain a pluralistic ideology.

In spite of this, as communicators of the Gospel, we must remain true to the contents of the message of the Gospel in order to avoid misperceptions about Christ as the only Lord and Savior. The author will relate at this point a personal experience shared by a colleague. Her related experience gives a practical example regarding how we communicate the gospel message in cross-cultural ministry (names of people and places will remain disclosed).

A certain Native community had received the gospel tent ministry that had returned to their village. One of the tribal members received Jesus into her life. Soon she began to understand the truths of the Gospel and expressed her desire to interpret sermons from the Word of God in the heart language of her people. She began to prepare in prayer and to study the scriptures while practicing the translation process of sermon delivery in her Native tongue.

In so doing, she came across the phrases from two specific scriptures: "born again" in John 3:3 and "new creation" from 2 Corinthians 5:17. She faced a dilemma. The wording in her Native tongue for both these phrases had to do with the belief of reincarnation. She realized that to use the very words in her language that denoted reincarnation teaching would cause confusion toward what the Bible teaches concerning being born again. It was at this point she began to pray for inspiration for the right use of words in her language in order to avoid this confusion.

Inspiration had come, and with excitement, she discovered a proper and more accurate word in her Native tongue that would help to interpret the English phrase for "born again" and "new creation" while not mislaying the biblical concept. This helped to avoid the confusion of reincarnation beliefs.

God knows the heart language of all people and will grant his servants the wisdom, discretion, and inspiration in our communication of the Gospel without confusion. This kind of guidance requires prayer, study, and meditation as we seek him.

We must never come across as though people do not have any knowledge of God.

Contextualization isn't always effective in the fact that there are times when people simply won't believe the Gospel as they feel confident in their world view, religious, traditional, and cultural practices. What are we to do? Like Paul, as he did in Athens, we move on. At times, we need to simply focus on those who are sincerely seeking for truth.

In some cases, during Paul's ministry, for example, at Lystra (see Acts 14:8–10), miracles authenticate the message. Miracles are a demonstration of the message of the Gospel. Often, need always prepares the heart to receive. Miracles confirm the message of the Gospel. Yet, when miracles do not occur, we can know that it is also within our lives where we embody the message which we believe.

Jesus is real. We must present the reality of his character as this also is in sync with the message we preach. Our changed life is much more than religious meditation but a changed life as a result of receiving the Gospel. Our own testimony reinforces the message we have believed and have allowed to shape our lives accordingly.

As believers in Christ, the Gospel is our worldview. We are the Gospel. This is why we must study the message of the Gospel and allow this to become our reality. We can be confident that the message of the Gospel does not change with the "changing tides" of today's cultures in all its ideals and constant altering trends. By being informed about the world view of others, we can understand how they view or interpret life and faith. With discretion, we can present the truths of the Gospel, starting with what knowledge they have about God and bridge them to Christ.

In turn, they themselves will begin developing a new world view in light of the Gospel. They will reevaluate what they have always known and begin to embrace the message we seek to communicate. The fundamentals in the message of the Gospel do not need to be compromised in its content in order to present its truths to the unconverted. In his series, *A Compassionate Call*, David Platt wrote:

> Christ's call in our lives is not to comfort in our culture. Christ in us actually compels us to counter our culture. Not to quietly sit and watch evolving cultural trends, and not to subtly shift our views amid changing cultural tides, but to courageously share and show our convictions through what we say and how we live, even (or especially) when these convictions contradict the popular positions of our day. And to do all of this not with conceited minds or calloused hearts, but with the humble compassion of Christ on constant display in everything we say and do.[107]

In view of cross-cultural ministry, we can understand that as believers, we are the influencers. We do not need to adjust our convictions and values in order to make the message appeasable to those which we are sent in order to proclaim a "relevant" or "contextualized" message. Susan Hyatt shares the following:

> In the same way that Jesus was not called to reflect the values of the culture into which He was born, the Church is not called to reflect of the values of the fallen culture. Instead, as Jesus

---

[107] Platt, David. *A Compassionate Call to Counter Culture in a World of Unreached People Groups*. Electronic Edition. Copyright 2015 by David Platt, Publisher, Tyndale House Publishers, Inc. USA, A Call To Counter Culture

demonstrated the values of heaven, the Church is to follow in his ways and demonstrate God's values in a fallen world.[108]

Our message—the Gospel—is what transforms the life of any person, no matter their culture. Culture does not and should not change our message, nor should it change our godly lifestyle.

---

[108] Hyatt, Susan C. *In the Spirit, We're Equal.* Copyright 1998 by Hyatt International Ministries, Inc. Publisher: Hyatt International Ministries, Inc. Dallas, Texas, pg. 268

13

All Believers Are Called

Paul conveys a bright privilege which we have as believers in Christ. He reflects in Romans 1:5 (NKJV) how that it is through Christ that "we have received grace and apostleship for obedience to the faith." As we read this, we understand that our initial source of authority and empowerment is through our relationship with Jesus Christ and his sending.

Paul finishes his statement that this commissioning is meant to be intersected "among all nations for his name," emphasizing the words "among all nations" to which this denotes a limitless Gospel mandate pertaining to a country, race, tribe, tongue, and gender in the fulfillment of the Great Commission. Simply said, the Gospel has no bounds.

We look again at the word *nations*; we find the original meaning: a race (as of the same habit), i.e. a tribe, specially a foreign (non-Jewish) one.[109] Our ministry of the spreading the Gospel message is meant for every individual believer to communicate without prejudice to any nationality. All believers have been given authorization by the Lord Jesus Christ to do so.

For those who favor the "spiritual jurisdiction view," as they believe that others are limited in carrying out the Gospel objectives

---

[109] Strong's Greek: ethnos G1484. *Olive Tree Enhanced Strong's Dictionary.* Copyright 1998–2018. Olive Tree Bible Software

among racial or tribal territories not of their own origin, is to imply that the Gospel of Jesus Christ is a racial or a tribal Gospel. The Gospel is not a White Man's Gospel, it is not a Native Gospel, it is not an African Gospel, it is not a Jewish Gospel, and so on.[110]

Including this is not a "gate keeper's" Gospel either. Although the Gospel transcends all cultures and it is certain that people of different cultures do present the Gospel of Jesus Christ, we need to be sure that we represent Christ and not our represented native culture. The Gospel is about Christ.

Paul, a Jew, was sent to many non-Jews, and his commissioning was from the Lord Jesus Christ. He was not a special case. At the close of Paul's statement in Romans 1:5, "[t]o whom you also are called," he gives recognition to these Roman believers that they also were called to the nations of the world as he. The principle brought to light reveals the conviction and compassion that we as believers must be compelled by in fulfilling our personal mission to which we have been entrusted by the Great Commissioner—Jesus Christ.

Although it is true that individuals sense a specific call to a specific country or people group, they are still not limited in ministering to other nationalities. As long as there is tenderness in the heart of those individuals, no matter their ethnicity, to hear the message of Gospel, we are obligated to share this good news to these who have an ear to hear, and we do so without partiality.

In our efforts of spreading the Good News, we are sobered with the reality of what has been entrusted to us. What a privilege! Kenneth E. Hagin wrote:

> Notice that after Jesus arose from the dead, He said, 'All power (or authority) is given unto me in heaven and in earth' (Matt. 28:18). Jesus immediately took the authority given to him in the earth and delegated it to his Body (Actually, the

---

[110] Smith, Craig. *White Man's Gospel.* Copyright 1997. Publisher: Indian Life Books, A Division of Indian Life Ministries, P.O. Box 3765, RPO Redwood Center, Winnipeg, Manitoba R2W 3R6 pp. 40–41

only way He could have authority on the earth—
He's not here—is through his Body).[111]

It is through us that the ministry of Christ will continue on this earth. It is God's heart that all nations would hear the Good News of Redemption. He is not concerned if the person who he has sent was or wasn't of the same skin color, gender, or birth origin of those being reached.

He wants all to hear. The call goes forth to all people to repent and believe the Gospel. Therefore, all believers are required to do their part in fulfilling the Great Commission.

It is a fact that in the natural, people generally respond to their own kind. All cultures are prone to relate with those of the same race; genders are likely to relate with the same gender; intellectuals will have more in common with other intellectuals; whatever class of society one comes from. In general, people are more comfortable with their own. That is human nature.

Grectchen Gaebelein Hull writes on ministering together as equals:

> Similarly, both men and women can fulfill roles of leadership, administrators, and teachers in the one Christian Body, and again they will do so in their individual ways. There is no reason to think God intended our mutual ruling or occupational function to be done in a unisex fashion. Men will bring a male perspective and women a female perspective. When both minister together—in line with their mutual creation in the image of God and in fulfillment of Jesus's prayer in John 17-20-

---

[111] Hagin, Kenneth E. *Paul's Revelation.* Electronic Edition Published 2013. Copyright ©1983. Publisher: Rhema Bible Church a.k.a. Kenneth Hagin Ministries, Inc. USA, Chapter 2

23—they will begin to mirror the unity, equality, harmony and cooperation of the Godhead.[112]

The reference above applies to not only gender issues but to all aspects of society for Christian ministry. The Gospel urges all believers to step outside out of their comfort zone with conviction that there are souls to be reached with his message. As the message of Christ's love is embodied in our lives, this enables us as his laborers to break through these barriers for the message to be received.

By filling each believer with the Holy Spirit,[113] God desires that his laborers would not be limited by the biases of others. As we are persistent in portraying the message of the Gospel, relying on his grace and wisdom to communicate this message, he will honor his Word by ministering to those who believe.

All believers have been given the power to witness.

It is a liberating truth to know that God has called all believers to share his love to a hurting world. In fact, if you love the Lord, in turn, you love the world. You have gained his love for the world. Daisy Washburn Osborn wrote:

> Jesus told his followers—women and men alike, 'You will receive power after that the Holy Ghost is come upon you and you shall be my witnesses' (Acts. 1:8). A witness simply tells what they have seen and what they know to be true. Every woman as well as every man can do that everywhere they go. Simply tell what you know to be true about Jesus. It really is that simple. The world is full of ordinary people who are hungry for a firsthand witness of Jesus Christ by an ordinary person. There is no such thing as a 'professional' witness of Christ. There are only PERSONAL witnesses

---

[112] Hull, Gretchen Gaebelein. *Equal to Serve.* Copyright by Gretchen Gaebelein Hull. Publisher: Baker Books, 1998, Grand Rapids, MI. 49516-6287, pg. 226

[113] Acts 1:8

and you are qualified to be on just as soon as you have a personal knowledge of Jesus as you Lord and Savior.[114]

Subsequently, understanding what it is that we have Christ in us, we ascertain that it is not necessary to measure ourselves with others. The scriptures teach that we are not wise when we compare ourselves with others:

> For we don't dare classify or compare ourselves with some who commend themselves. But in measuring themselves by themselves and comparing themselves to themselves, they lack understanding. (2 Cor. 10:12, HCSB).

Another translation states this same verse in this fashion:

> Oh, don't worry, I wouldn't dare say that I am as wonderful as these other men who tell you how good they are! Their trouble is that they are only comparing themselves with each other and measuring themselves against their own little ideas. What stupidity! (2 Cor. 10:12, The Living Bible)

It is not wise to get caught up in comparing ourselves with others. Neither is it wise to compare one minister over another, especially based on their race, gender, status, education, wealth, or natural birth origin. As equals in the body of Christ, we have been given the same measure of faith, "[t]o everyone who is among you, not to think of himself more highly than he ought to think, but to think soberly, as God has dealt to each one a measure of faith" (Romans 12:3, NKJV).

---

[114] Osborn, Daisy Washburn. *Five Choices for Women Who Win*. Copyright 2004 by LaDonna C. Osborn. Publisher: Osborn Ministries Intl., Tulsa, OK. 74102, pp. 156–157

This measure of faith was not given in preference to what we are in the natural.

Instead, it is given based on what we are in the new creation identity as we continue to remain in faith in Christ. Our confidence comes from knowing who we are in Christ and the assurance we have of the message which he sent us to proclaim—his Gospel.

> Then Peter replied, "I see very clearly that God shows no favoritism. In every nation he accepts those who fear him and do what is right." (Acts 10:34–35, NLT)

God is not preferable toward the biological factors of one person over another, be it racial or gender-based. His Holy Spirit comes to fill each one as they trust in Christ to be their Savior, and then he equips each believer to continue the ministry of Christ here on earth. In her book, *Women and Self Esteem*, Daisy Washburn Osborn wrote:

> Being a woman does not change me from being a believer, a disciple of Jesus Christ, his follower, his servant. What He said to all believers, He says to me—and to you also. his Great Commission applies to women the same as to men. The power of the Holy Spirit in a woman's life is no different than it is in a man's life.[115]

The statement quoted above has much "food for thought," which not only applies to gender issues, but this truth can be applied to ethnic issues as well in the same way that being a believer does not change our gender—male or female—therefore, being a believer also does not change who we are ethnically. What transpires inwardly is the heart that believes the truths of redemption, and we are changed from within, we are conformed to the image of Christ. Jesus com-

---

[115] Osborn, Daisy Wasburn. *Women & Self Esteem.* Copyright 2008 by LaDonna C. Osborn. Publisher: Osborn Ministries Intl. Tulsa, OK. 74102, pg. 23

manded his disciples: "Make disciples of all nations" (Mt. 28:19, NKJV). There were no indications in his instructions that this commissioning to the nations of the world was dependent on our genetics.

Years ago, as I was attending a church in a small community, I heard the Mission's Committee Coordinator speak simply, yet with wisdom, "Every heart without Jesus, a mission field. Every heart with Jesus, a missionary."

This left a lasting impression on me and still convicts me to this day. Our commissioning is contingent on our being made new creations, being filled with the Holy Spirit, and being sent by his Spirit. It is through our response of obedience to him that we are empowered to be his witnesses as we share the message of redemption—the Gospel—to this hurting world.

14

In His Name—The Message
of Conviction

Previously, we have reviewed the basis of our spiritual authority in Christ is located within the realities of the spiritual new birth. This encompasses that through faith in Christ, all believers are made citizens of heaven, included in his covenant, have attained righteousness by faith in Christ, and by this, we have equal privilege to pray. We have also portrayed the concept of biblical equality observed in the truths of redemption. All believers in Christ are called to continue his ministry, no matter our backgrounds. That focusing on these truths keeps us in line with the message of the Gospel when we begin to minister across cultural barriers.

We will now observe the importance of holding true to the message which we have been entrusted and what it means to represent Christ in this world as we go forth in his name.

Holding True to the Gospel Message

The reason for Paul's letters to the numerous churches was not merely for sending a newsletter greeting to his faithful supporting flock, like so many ministries practice today to raise support. In fact, Paul was in jail as he wrote most of these letters. As we read his epistles, we find what motivated him to write these letters. He was concerned that the believers in the places where he established churches were losing sight of the message of the Gospel. To state a few:

> Hold fast to the pattern of sound words which you have heard from me, in faith and love which are in Christ Jesus. That good thing which was committed to you, keep by the Holy Spirit who dwell in us. (2 Tim. 1:12–14, NKJV)

> Now this I say lest anyone should deceive you with persuasive words. (Col. 2:4, NKJV)

> Let the word of Christ dwell in you richly. (Col. 3:16, NKJV)

> I marvel that you are turning away so soon from him who called you in the grace of Christ to a different gospel, which is not another; but there are some who trouble you and want to pervert the gospel of Christ. But even if we, or an angel from heaven, preach any other gospel to you than what we have preached to you, let him be accursed. As we have said before, so now I say again, if anyone preaches any other gospel to you that what you have received, let him be accursed...O foolish Galatians! Who has bewitched you that you should not obey the truth before whose eyes Jesus Christ was clearly portrayed among you as crucified? (Galatians 1:6–9, 3:1, NKJV)

These are just a few examples in some of his epistles which reveal his concern for these believers to continue in the Word of the Gospel of Redemption. In his first letter to the Thessalonians, he describes how they were impacted upon their receiving of God's Word:

> [w]hen you received the word of God which you heard from me, you welcomed it not as the word of men, but as it is truth, the word of God which also effectively works in you who believe. (1 Thess. 2:13b, NKJV)

What was it that worked so effectively among them? And why? It was the Word of God which they had come to believe, and their lives were wonderfully revolutionized at their reception of the Gospel. Paul's concern for the believers was that they were drifting from the very source that impacted their lives. In his attempt to write to them personally, he reminds them of the fundamentals of their faith in Christ. We benefit today from these epistles today.

Rick Renner briefs about the digression of the Word of God that began to occur not long after the first century believer's era and the results that transpired. He warns believers today of the reason people do not discern false teaching is due to not prioritizing the Word of God. In his book, *Merchandising the Anointing*, he wrote:

> But eventually, this drifting away from the Word became so gross, so far removed from the message the apostles preached, so far off into strange and curious teachings, that there was no longer enough Word being preached for the Holy Spirit to confirm… The strong presence of the Spirit was attached to the strong teaching of the Word. When the Word was gone, the Spirit's power was gone too…Therefore if we want power, we must learn a lesson from history and stick to the Word. These two—The Word and power—are inseparable.[116]

---

[116] Renner, Rick. *Merchandising the Anointing—Developing Discernment for These Last Days*. Copyright ©1990 by Rick Renner Ministries. Publisher: Albury

The Word of God is the voice of authority in our lives and ministry, for it is by the hearing of God's Word that we have faith. "Faith comes by hearing, and hearing by the Word of God" (Romans 10:17, NKJV) and, "The Gospel is the power of God unto salvation" (Roman 1:16, NKJV). How can one receive and know salvation if they do not hear word of the Gospel? How can we remain in our newfound freedom in Christ if we do not hold fast to the message of the Gospel?

The Gospel is the word of reconciliation of which we are stewards of seeing that God has "committed to us the word of reconciliation" (2 Cor. 5:19, NKJV); and "we have been approved by God to be entrusted with the gospel" (1Th. 2:4, NKJV). We will be held accountable before God for the use of the message, which we have been given to proclaim. We must take care not to allow its message to be tainted and communicate it as the Bible proclaims it.

The Gospel is the foundation to all that we believe. "For no other foundation can anyone lay than that which is laid, which is Jesus Christ" (1 Cor. 3:11, NKJV). We must always refer back to our foundation in order to keep our lives and ministry in sync with the message of the Gospel. In his book, *Seducing Spirits and Doctrines of Demons*, Rick Renner also wrote:

> You can't give enough foundation to the Church. As long as babies are being born, they're going to need foundation… God is very interested in foundation-laying. Yes, we've got to move beyond foundation; but, saints, we've always got to come back to it. It is the basis for everything else, and where there is no foundation, the structure is going to fall.[117]

Publishing, Tulsa, OK. 74147-0406, pg.106
[117] Renner, Rick. *Seducing Spirits and Doctrines of Demons*. Copyright 1998 by Rick Renner Ministries. Publisher: Albury Publishing, Tulsa, OK. 74147-0406 pg. 119

There is no revelation outside of the founding truths of redemption. Paul spoke of this foundation "having been built upon the foundation of the apostles and prophets, Jesus Christ Himself the chief cornerstone" (Ephesians 2:20, NKJV). Dr. LaDonna Osborn wrote:

> I re-emphasize that the knowledge of redemption is the foundation of all spiritual revelation. Christian doctrine is to be evaluated by and be consistent with the underlying and overarching revelation of the gospel of redemption.[118]

This foundation of redemption is about the revelation of Jesus. This now takes us to the question which Jesus asked his disciples, "'Who do men say that I am?' So, they said, 'Some say John the Baptist, some Elijah and others Jeremiah or one of the prophets.' He said to them, 'Who do you say that I am?'" (Matthew 16:13–15, NKJV). This is still a valid question today. Do we know who Jesus is? Do we know his place?

Peter gave Jesus the right answer as it came to him by revelation, "You are the Christ, the Son of the living God" (vs. 16, NKJV). The foundation of the apostles and prophets is the revelation of Jesus, who he is, and his position. Christ's ministry was not similar in task to that of the Old Testament ministries. Today, his message is not an "add-on" to a system we are familiarized with. Neither is his message additional to a worldview of those who do not know the Gospel. Instead, his message changes our viewpoint. His message replaces the former. Christ is the foundation to our faith, the ministry, and message to which he has graciously granted us.

When we realize his position, then we too will come to know our place. Our lives begin to conform to his ways; our worldviews change as we grasp the message of the Gospel.

Jesus responds to Peter's answer, "[f]lesh and blood has not revealed this to you, but My Father who is in heaven…on this rock, I

---

[118] Osborn, LaDonna C. *God's Big Picture*. Copyright 2001 by LaDonna C. Osborn. Publisher: Osborn Publishers, Tulsa, OK. 74102, pg. 31

will build My church, and the gates of Hades shall not prevail against it" (vv. 17–18, NKJV). This speaks to us about the understanding that we have of who Jesus is, which is pictured as a rock. Jesus was not talking about a decoration which in many homes, properties, and businesses of today have where a rock is placed along a driveway or in a yard. The concept of a "rock" in those times would mean a foundational center to which held a building structure together, a chief cornerstone. Without that cornerstone, nothing will hold together. The disciples knew what Jesus indicated by stating "[u]pon this rock, I will build My church."

The foundation of the apostles' ministry was not in the signs, wonders, and miracles, although it did prove them. Nor did they ever claim their foundation of spiritual authorization was due to their natural birth culture and earthly achievements. Instead, their foundation was in their revelation of Jesus, which empowered them for ministry. They went forth, knowing that he is the one who holds all things together. Christ is the core of our values and belief system of our faith. He is the center of our lives. He is the main theme in the entire message of the Bible. He is the revelation of God the Father. Without a revelation of Jesus, we are missing the whole point.

Without him, we are not able to overcome. "[u]pon this rock I will build My church and the gates of Hades will not prevail against it" (vs. 18b, NKJV). The gates of Hades (hell) will not prevail against those who are founded on the rock, Jesus Christ. It will not prevail against those who have a revelation of Jesus, those who have a revelation of who they are in Christ, those who are dependent upon the indwelling of his Spirit in their lives to do the task to which he has called each one. These are those who the gates of hell cannot stop, no matter how hard the enemy tries. These are those who do not claim to have a source of spiritual authority in themselves apart from their knowledge of Jesus. These are also those who continue in their revelation of Jesus. Our revelation knowledge of Jesus will keep us solidified in the face of adversity with joy.

We must not be moved away from the hope of the Gospel, "But you must continue to believe this truth, stand firmly in it…don't drift away from the assurance" (Colossians 1:23, NLT). It is crucial that we pay attention to what is being taught in Christian gatherings. If what is being emphasized is not centered on the biblical revelation of Jesus, then we are to simply not pay attention to it.

> [h]old on to the pattern of wholesome teach-
> ing…through the power of the Holy Spirit who
> lives within us, carefully guard the precious truth
> that has been entrusted you (1 Timothy 1:13,14,
> NLT)

> [w]e were bold in our God to speak to you the
> gospel of God in much conflict. For our exhorta-
> tion did not come from error or uncleanness nor
> was it in deceit. But as we have been approved
> by God to be entrusted with the gospel, even so
> we speak, not as pleasing men, but God who test
> our hearts. For neither at any time did we use
> flattering words, as you know, nor a cloak for
> covetousness—God is witness. Nor did we seek
> glory from men…we preached to you the gospel
> of God. (1 Thessalonians 2:2b–6,8b, NKJV)

Paul understood the purpose of his calling. He understood his purpose was not to promote his culture, his ministry, name, or to build a reputation for himself. His intention was not to flatter them to gain their favor. His conviction was that he had been entrusted with the message of the Gospel.

We need to understand that the message of the Gospel is not the message of man. It is the message of God to this lost and dying world. It is the only message that works. It is the only message that brings true deliverance and healing to individual lives, families, and societies. God will confirm his word and not the word of man.

> For our gospel did not come to you in word only,
> but also in power and in the Holy Spirit and in
> much assurance. (1 Thessalonians 1:5a)

If we want the manifested anointing of God's Spirit upon our ministry, then we must preach the message of the Gospel of his kingdom. This is exemplified in the ministry of the disciples as we observe their example in the book of Acts. And truly, God confirmed his Word with power. Again, he will not confirm the word of man. Paul could boldly say:

> For I am not ashamed of the Gospel of Christ for
> it is the power of God unto salvation for every-
> one who believes...for in it the righteousness
> of God is revealed from faith to faith. (Romans
> 1:16a–17a, NKJV)

God's power is manifested at the preaching of the Gospel of Christ. His power is not revealed in our self-acclamation of who or what we are in the natural. The release of his power is in conjunction with the proclamation of the message of the Gospel among those who hear and believe it. It is Christ in us, the hope of glory (Colossians 1:27). As stated before, it is not our ethnic or gender identity that is the hope of glory; rather, it is Christ himself.

"The righteousness of God is revealed from faith to faith" (Romans 1:17, NKJV). The more we preach the message of the Gospel of Christ, the more we understand his righteousness. His righteousness is revealed upon the preaching of the Gospel of Christ.

The writer, as a tribal member, cannot reveal the power of God or the righteousness of God through expressing her native identity. To do so only represents herself and not him who saved her. According to scripture, the writer is responsible to preach only the message of the Gospel and to represent him. The writer no longer represents her cultural nationality. The writer identifies with Christ.

In summary, teaching the truths of redemption sheds light upon the revelation of who we are in Christ in his righteousness as we continue preaching and teaching of the Gospel of Christ.

> For whoever is ashamed of Me and My Words in
> this adulterous and sinful generation, of him the

Son of Man also will be ashamed when He comes in the glory of his Father with the holy angels. (Mark 3:38, NKJV)

This scripture would seem like strong words that Jesus used. Yet, with these words, we are challenged that not being ashamed of his words is not a mere suggestion. In other words, he desires for us to remain confident in him and the message he has trusted us with. We are often tempted to accept that it is more effective to continue identifying with culture and the ideals of trendy style. When we do this, we are actually losing confidence in who we are in Christ and his Words. We do not show faith in him or his Words. We give in to the fear of man and bring shame to his name. His message becomes unclear by our very actions when we prioritize what is fashionable. Not being ashamed means to remain confident in the message of the Gospel.

God is who he says he is, "[h]e who comes to God must believe that He is" (Hebrews 11:6, NKJV). It is not necessary to make the message of the Gospel fit the pattern of this world in order to appease the world. Instead, we can remain confident that Jesus is alive. He is the power and the wisdom of God. He is the revelation of the Father. He is our way to salvation. He is the way, the truth, and the life, and no one can go to the Father except through him. There is no greater revelation than Jesus Christ himself. There is no greater message to proclaim than Jesus Christ himself. There is no other name given among men to save us. He is the Word of Life.

Today, many are caught up in the latest "prophetic message." However, the Bible teaches that Holy Spirit testifies of Jesus, "But when the Helper comes, whom I shall send to you from the Father, the Spirit of truth who proceeds from the Father, He will testify of Me" (John 15:26, NKJV). Many today overlook that Jesus is the fulfilled prophetic message, "for the testimony of Jesus is the spirit of prophecy" (Revelations 19:10c, NKJV). He is the fulfillment of the Word of God.

The Holy Spirit will never steer us away from the testimony of Christ. He will always bring us to our foundation, and there we ascertain our values as we align our convictions with what he teaches us in his Word. Through his word, we discover our true identity, and his Holy Spirit will teach us how to represent him in this world.

15

"In His Name"—What that Means

Jesus gave an important key for his followers. This key is seldom lost sight of. Many in Christian ministry today are concerned about relevancy and begin to err in their ministry endeavors by attempting to contextualize cultural ideologies with Christian ministry. The attempt to contextualize has brought confusion as to what the message was about and who was the focus.

The intentions in being relevant were done by highlighting an individual's natural birth culture, deeming it significant to authorization for ministry to those of the same culture. Sadly, it is believed that by representing one's nationality, this will give license to operate in spiritual authority, based on who they are in their birth culture. However, when it comes to operating in spiritual authority, this approach of cultural identification is the wrong key.

As stated throughout this volume, only a proper understanding of redemption will enable all believers to operate in true spiritual authority in the revelation of who we are in Christ. The key that unlocks this ability is to rest by faith in the power of his name.

As we have also stated earlier, Jesus came to redeem mankind from the dominion of Satan. Jesus made his words clear, "All authority has been given to me in heaven and on earth. Go therefore and make disciples of all the nations, baptizing them in the name of the Father and of the Son and of the Holy Spirit" (Matthew 28:18–19, NKJV). We are to go forth "in the name of." We do not go forth representing our natural birth identity, but we are to go with confidence in the name of Jesus, acknowledging that our own name and identity has no power over the devil's territory.

Name defined: a name (literally or figuratively; authority, character).[119]

From this definition, we conclude that we represent the authority and character of Christ as we are sent to go in his name. When we represent Christ, we reveal his authority and character. People may see our flesh in the natural, but they will realize that it is because of Christ's anointing and faith in his name that people are saved, delivered, and healed. "It is not that we are competent in ourselves to consider anything as coming from ourselves, but our competence is from God" (2 Cor. 3:5, HCSB). With that in mind, Paul also continues, "But we have this treasure in earthen vessels, that the excellency of the power may be of God and not of us" (2 Cor. 4:7, NKJV). We cannot acclaim anything to ourselves but the name of Jesus.

We minister in his name:

Jesus said, "[i]n My Name..." (Mark 16:17b, NKJV). In his name, we can go forth in the power of his Spirit to minister the Gospel. He also said that we are to make disciples of all nations, baptizing them "in the name of the Father and of the Son and of the Holy Spirit" (Matthew 28:19, NKJV). It is in his name that we are to make disciples, not according to the names of our ministries. As believers, we are to be identified with his name both in our personal and public lives. No other name is given under heaven by which man should be saved (Acts 4:12).

In fact, we read in the book of Acts how the disciples exercised ministering in his name. For example, Peter and John met a lame man on the way into the temple to pray. They boldly said to the lame man, "Silver and gold I do not have, but what I do have I give you: In the name of Jesus Christ of Nazareth, rise up and walk" (Acts 3:6, NKJV). I wonder what the results would be had they

---

[119] Strong's number g3686: ὄνομα onoma; from 1832: *Olive Tree Enhanced Strong's Dictionary*. Copyright 1998–2017. Olive Tree Bible Software

used their own names. "I am Peter, a follower of Jesus, now rise up and walk." They did not use their own identity, nor had they shown confidence in who they were in themselves. They obviously took the words of Jesus to heart and ministered in his name. How simple, yet so powerful.

Peter and John faced opposition for ministering in the name of Jesus. In Acts chapter four, they were brought before the Sanhedrin after they had been taken into custody. The council asked, "By what power or by what name have you done this?" (Acts 4:7, NKJV). They were not interested in their personal names. They were strongly opposed to the name of Jesus, for they knew of his ministry in light of the numerous miracles which he performed.

They must've have known that this name had significance and power. The devil was obviously behind this, influencing their envious hearts to try to stop them. The devil will oppose any believer who ministers in the name of Jesus. The world also will not acknowledge the name of Jesus as the means of salvation and truth. The world is under the influence of Satan who opposes the kingdom of God. He knows there is authority in the name of Jesus.

Peter knew who to give the credit to and would not take the glory to himself as he boldly replies to their question:

> Let it be known to you all and to all the people of Israel, that by the name of Jesus Christ of Nazareth, whom you crucified, whom God raised from the dead, by him this man stands here before you whole. (Acts 4:10, NKJV).

The threats they received from the council did not stop them, for they had a revelation in ministering in the power of his name (see Acts 4:13–19). The book of Acts is a source which we can glean from the examples of these early believers. Truly, they practiced the simple principle of ministering in his name. The gates of hell could not stop them, for they walked in the revelation of Jesus—who he is (his character) and his position (his authority).

We meet together in his name:

For where two or three of you are gathered
together in my name, I am there in the midst of
them. (Matthew 18:20, NKJV)

There are many kinds of gatherings which take place in the
realm of Christian ministry today. It is from conferences, seminars,
workshops, regular church services, Bible studies, celebrations, cru-
sades, outreaches, and the like which are happening everywhere. The
Church at large is very busy. Certain rallies are intended to focus
"prophetically" for the ethnic expression of each individual culture
represented. It is within these kinds of gatherings where the "spiritual
jurisdiction view" is accepted.

In turn, this kind of gathering becomes an assembling unto the
culture of highlight. Who then is being lifted up? Who is the meeting
centered on? They say it's about Jesus, when in reality, he is not given
the preeminence.

It is at these kinds of meetings where much confusion has
spread for those who struggle in seeking to find who they are. Instead
of being taught to focus on the new creation identity in Christ, they
are misled that their significance is centered on their natural birth
as they are also misinformed that this gives them ample spiritual
authority in their respective communities. As a result, this kind of
gathering focuses on their natural birth identity, and faith becomes
misplaced—a wrong foundation has been laid. This becomes a dis-
advantage to these individuals as they are given the wrong impression
about their role in Christian ministry.

However, this cannot be dealt with by direct contesting of these
trendy ideals that have been accepted. The best response to this is to
simply teach the proper truths of redemption and redirect the focus
of the believers' identity in Christ. As we consistently keep the standard of lifting up the name of Jesus, we exemplify that preeminence
is given to One who is worthy of our worship. We also personify
gathering in his name to which his presence manifests among those
who are sincerely seeking him.

As we congregate, our faith fixates that as we gather in his name, we experience a corporate anointing of his glorious presence, "you also, as living stones, are being built up a spiritual house, a royal priesthood, to offer up spiritual sacrifices to God through Jesus Christ" (1 Peter 2:5, NKJV); "in whom you also are being built together for a dwelling place of God in the Spirit" (Ephesians 2:22, NKJV). Meeting together in his name will release an anointed outpouring of the tangible presence of the Holy Spirit, and this is not dependent upon those certain participants who represent their birth culture.

Rather, it is due to the common ground of all believers in their sincere faith in Christ as Jesus said, "The hour is coming, and now is, when the true worshippers will worship that Father in spirit and truth; for the Father is seeking such to worship him" (John 4:24, NKJV). True worshippers of the Father are those whose eyes are fixed on him who redeemed us with his blood; this is the One whom they are worshipping.

We pray in his name:

> And whatsoever ye shall ask in my name, that I will do that the Father may be glorified in the Son. If ye shall ask anything in my name, I will do it (John 14:13–14, NKJV)

First, we are instructed that in our asking, we are to do so in his name. As a tribal member and yet follower of Christ, since the writer understands which birth that counts, she learns to pray in the name of Jesus. The writer does not acclaim rights to pray in certain lands, because she is from there. Rather, it is because of faith in Jesus's name that brings results. The faith of the writer as she is praying is not resting in her natural birth identity, but simply, it is faith in the name of Jesus alone.

> [t]hat whatsoever ye shall ask of the Father in my name, He may give it you. (John 16:16, NKJV)

The writer's ability to pray to the Father is not sourced in her representing culture. The Father will honor the prayer of the believer who knows their righteousness is of him and those whose faith is in the name of Jesus. The writer does not see any supporting teachings of Jesus indicated within his instructions on prayer that his disciples were to be asking in the name (authority and character) of their natural birth. When we acclaim that the participation of individuals from certain locales are the reason for divine blessing due to their natural birth culture, it is to negate these words of Jesus:

> And in that day ye shall ask me nothing. Verily, verily, I say unto you, Whatsoever ye shall ask the Father in my name, he will give it you. Hitherto have ye asked nothing in my name: ask, and ye shall receive, that your joy may be full.
>
> These things have I spoken unto you in proverbs: but the time cometh, when I shall no more speak unto you in proverbs, but I shall shew you plainly of the Father. At that day ye shall ask in my name: and I say not unto you, that I will pray the Father for you. (John 16:23–26, NKJV).

How often do we as a church miss the key principle of praying in his name? Too often, ministers or ministries go forth in their own name, implying that their spiritual authority rests on the representation of themselves. No one is a power unto themselves. Only Jesus holds that power and authority. He holds the keys. Simply, spiritual authority only rests in Jesus's name, granting us right or jurisdiction to minister. Our racial identity does not grant us legal authority to minister, preach, pray, or prophesy.

Peter exemplified this: "Look at us...silver and gold I do not have, but what I do have I give you, In the name of Jesus Christ of Nazareth, rise up and walk" (Acts 3:4,6, NKJV). We must value what we have in his name above all that people would deem as significant. No amount of money could have helped the man who received his miracle that day. Peter's male Jewishness did not transfer healing power. It was faith in the name of Jesus alone.

Jesus gave instruction to our position in asking.

Results are what we as ministers of the gospel are often seeking in our ministry efforts. By the same token, it is not only we ourselves who are watching for results; so also is the Lord of the Harvest. He wants results as well. Jesus taught us the key to achieving that goal:

> Abide in Me and I in you. As the branch cannot bear fruit of itself, unless it abides in the vine, neither can you, unless you abide in Me. I am the vine; you are the branches. He who abides in Me and I in him bears much fruit; for without Me you can do nothing. If anyone does not abide in Me, he is cast out as a branch and is withered; and they gather them and throw them in the fire and they are burned. If you abide in me and my words abide in you, you will ask what you desire and it shall be done for you. By this my Father is glorified, that you bear much fruit; so you will be My disciples. (John 15:4–8, NKJV)

Jesus taught that as his followers, we must practice the art of abiding in him and in his words. Therein lies the secret to our asking. Abiding in him simply means to take time to draw from his Spirit the spiritual resources, strength, wisdom, power, and anointing we need as harvest workers. Jesus's words were very clear: "Apart from me, you can do nothing" (vs.5, NKJV). We must accept this truth. Apart from him, we can do nothing.

As a believer, the writer understands that if she is not abiding in Jesus who is the Vine, then she has nothing to give as far as Christian ministry and growth is concerned. However, since she is born again, this automatically joins her to the Vine as she learns to abide in him and his words. From the position of abiding, she is able to ask of the Father in the name of Jesus, and she knows he will answer her request.

In summary, the purpose in the believer's abiding is that the believer learns to tune into the Fathers heart as his love motivates each believer to win the lost. This simple yet profound truth reveals to us that one cannot acclaim anything to themselves when the fruit, which Jesus spoke about, begins to produce. We are not a source unto ourselves.

In truth, we cannot make ourselves into new creations in Christ. It is God who does this work, "For it is God work in you both to will and to do for his good pleasure" (Philippians 2:13, NKJV). Since we know that as we have accepted Christ into our lives, his Spirit comes into us, and we are born again. We understand that through our relationship with him, we begin to produce the life of Christ as we learn to cultivate our new faith in him through his Word, prayer, and worship. This is a gift of God's grace granted to the one who has faith in him:

> For by grace you have been saved though faith and that not of yourselves; it is the gift of God, not of works, lest anyone should boast. For we are his workmanship, created in Christ Jesus for good works, which God prepared beforehand that we should walk in him. (Ephesians 2:8–10, NKJV).

Bearing much fruit comes from our ability to abide in him as we each develop an intimate fellowship with the Lord, his grace empowers us for good works. We are able to pray with faith in his name because of the assurance we have developed in him. No believer can claim that prayer results occur because they represent their culture or that this gives them spiritual authority to pray.

Jesus taught us that it is within our abiding in him that when we ask the Father in his name, it shall be done. There are no hidden clues in what Jesus taught that needs dissecting to find any further claims for answered prayer other than what we find that faith in his name and our constant abiding in him, which is the crucial part.

In the last two chapters, we have given a two-fold explanation of what it means to represent Christ. His Name and his message are our source of conviction which cannot be altered by the trendy and yet constant changes of today's culture. God and his word never change (see Psalm 119:89).

16

Conclusion

We have addressed the "spiritual jurisdiction view" with careful study of the scriptures and research as the author has responded to this trendy, yet misconceived ideology. We also encompassed throughout this volume the biblical view of being born again, our redeemed status, that all nations (ethnic groups) are included in his covenant through faith in Christ.

We have presented the concept of biblical equality. We have also defined biblical spiritual authority, righteousness, and our redeemed identity in Christ. We have reviewed how spiritual authority in Christ applies for every believer. We have expounded what the Bible teaches about our position to pray and what it means to go forth in his name as we remain true to his message. We have emphasized refocusing on the fundamentals of Christian faith, which brings correction to our thinking of whether we should we sway from the core values and beliefs of the Gospel.

We will conclude with two examples: First, we will observe how Jesus handled being questioned about his authority and his conduct toward those who operated in false authority who questioned him. Secondly, we will also observe John the Baptist's example, finally concluding with the necessity for the true message of the Gospel to come forth as this is the only message that works.

They Questioned Jesus's Authority

Now it happened on one of those days, as He taught the people in the temple and preached the gospel, that the chief priests and the scribes, together with the elders, confronted him and spoke to him, saying, "Tell us, by what authority are You doing these things? Or who is he who gave You this authority?" But He answered and said to them, "I also will ask you one thing, and answer Me: The baptism of John—was it from heaven or from men?"

And they reasoned among themselves, saying, "If we say, 'From heaven,' He will say, 'Why then did you not believe him?' But if we say, 'From men,' all the people will stone us, for they are persuaded that John was a prophet." So they answered that they did not know where it was from. And Jesus said to them, "Neither will I tell you by what authority I do these things." (Luke 20:1–8, NKJV)

Earlier in this review, we related to these scriptures as we have defined biblical authority. The writer will now begin to highlight the core attitude that confronted Jesus in this passage of scripture. It is interesting that the authority of Jesus was questioned by these religious leaders of the time he walked as a man on this earth. The heart of the matter was the disposition which the chief priest, scribes, and elders held toward him.

In the stronghold of their minds, there were prejudices, jealousies, insecurities, and pride. They felt threatened. They simply did not want to acknowledge him. These attitudes are similar in our day among those who harbor prejudice and racist mindsets toward those who are not "one of them." However, the Lord's response was filled with wisdom in that he did not need to answer to them. He knew who he was. Yet, in another place in Matt. 28:18, he informs his disciples, "All authority has been given to me in heaven and on earth...."

The reason he discloses with his disciples where his authority came from was that they accepted his authority as one sent from God. Due to their faith in him, they received delegation to continue his work after his departure. This delegation was not limited to these twelve since this also applies to all followers of Christ today. What we learn from this example: Those who accept the one sent from God will be recipients of the divine blessing of the Gospel that they come with.

Paul wrote to the believers in Rome, "I know that when I come to you, I shall come in the fullness of the blessing of the gospel of Christ," (Romans 15:19, NKJV). The Gospel comes with the divine blessing of heaven. This divine blessing is dispersed upon the proclamation of the Gospel and is not conditional to the ethnicities of a person's genetics.

Spiritual discernment is needed as we open our hearts to these sent ministries as we do not want to reject the ones that God sends. However, to avoid making the mistake of rejection, we err by readily accepting what these ministries pronounce without the filter of God's Word. Although we, as generations before, within the Body of Christ of today, we realize that we will often contend with the false teachings of false prophets and false teachers. How do we discern if their message is from God?

Rick Renner highlights Peter's expressed concern seen in 2 Peter 2:1 regarding false prophets and false teachers. The author has found his observations taken from the Greek word, a study on the word *teacher* to be insightful and noteworthy:

> You must understand that both the prophet and teacher "teach" to some degree. The purpose of both of these gifts is to "revelate" truth to the Church. They both stand as "revelators." So when Peter says, 'even as there shall be false teachers among you' he is lumping all 'revelators' together—whether they are prophets, teachers,

apostles, evangelist or pastors. All of these gifts stand as 'revelators' inside the Church. Therefore, to be technically correct, we must understand that Peter is not specifically predicting a prophet or a teacher problem. Rather, he is predicting a 'revelator' problem! Any of the fivefold ministry gifts could potentially be included here. Also notice that this problem today is simply a repeat from the Old Testament. Just as the Old Testament saints had a psuedoprophetes crisis, or a 'pretend prophet' crisis, Peter declares that we shall have pseudodaskalos crisis, or a 'pretend revelators' crisis to deal with in the last days. Whether you call these revelators prophets or teachers, the problem is one and the same. The issue is false revelation coming forth from people who are forcing themselves into spiritual positions which God did not give them. Thus, I have come to call them 'the great pretenders.'[120]

This is what we are dealing with regarding the very issue, which the author has addressed that these speakers who share "revelations" in keeping with the "spiritual jurisdiction view" have spoken in error. The error which was made was not in their encouragement toward Indigenous believers to arise in their calling. However, the error is located within the insinuation that these Indigenous believers have special rank in the geographical districts which they are from.

This has brought on a misapplication about their spiritual authority. This also explains why the misconception about their role in Christian ministry. The author believes it has been spoken in error, because this trendy view claims "special revelation," yet is found to not be harmonious with scripture in light of biblical equality and

[120] Renner, Rick. *Merchandising the Anointing—Developing Discernment for These Last Days.* Copyright 1990 by Rick Renner Ministries. Publisher: Albury Publishing, Tulsa, OK. 74147-0406, pp. 178–179

redemption. Instead, the outcome of this teaching has brought further discrimination and division.

Not only had Paul dealt with discrimination, he also dealt with
sectarianism. Earlier, we discussed how Jesus corrected his followers
touching this kind of attitude. In his first letter, Paul wrote to the
Corinthian believers:

> Now I have applied all this [about parties and
> factions] to myself and Apollos for your sakes,
> brethren, so that from what I have said of us [as
> illustrations], you may learn [to think of men in
> accordance with Scripture and] not to go beyond
> that which is written, that none of you may be
> puffed up and inflated with pride and boast
> in favor of one [minister and teacher] against
> another.
>
> For who separates you from the others [as
> a faction leader]? [Who makes you superior and
> sets you apart from another, giving you the pre-
> eminence?] What have you that was not given to
> you? If then you received it [from someone], why
> do you boast as if you had not received [but had
> gained it by your own efforts]? (1 Corinthians
> 4:6–7, AMPC)

The difference between singularizing groups over another and
teaching the truths of redemption is found in that the former fos-
ters division, and the latter produces unity, equality, and mutuality
among God's people. Our duty is joyous, yet somber, to all the more
preach and teach the Gospel of Redemption as we seek to continually focus on our true identity in Christ. Doing so will arm those we
teach in the Body of Christ with truth and will also enable hearers to
recognize false teaching.

There are no magic formulas. The only solution for this world
and including the church is the refocus on the Gospel of Jesus Christ.
Several minsters who are now in the presence of Jesus have stated their

THE BIRTH THAT COUNTS

concern regarding the message of the Gospel being put aside. Will it continue to be vocalized in future generations? The writer believes that concern needs to be ours today. Freda Lyndsay was among those concerned for the church of today as she wrote:

> There is a whole world full of 'our generation,' many of whom were reared by godless parents, who in turn were subject to the same lack of spiritual training. As we reflect on the end of this millennium and the coming of the next, we see a world steeped in corruption and unable to solve its own problems. A death-producing agenda lies before us. The best way to understand the present and prepare for the future is to turn to the Scriptures.[121]

Again, this needs to be our concern today. Relating a recent personal experience during a Gospel outreach, the writer and her coworker were ministering in a certain community in Canada. A children's meetings had been held in the home of a local believer. The house was packed with youth.

Before we introduced the Gospel, being as it was nearing the Christmas season, we asked the children if any of them had ever heard about the Nativity, not expecting blank stares. To our astonishment, only two of the twelve attending the children's meeting were familiar with story of Mary, Joseph, and the baby Jesus.

With enthusiasm, we exclaimed, "We'd love to be the first to tell you!"

This experience was not thirty years ago; this was only recently in December of 2017. The writer is alarmed that so many youths within the North American continent do not know the true Christmas story. It is a sin that this generation does not know the true Gospel.

---

[121] Lindsay, Freda. *The Second Wind.* Copyright ©1999, Christ for the Nations. Publisher: Christ for the Nations, Dallas, TX. 75376-9000 pg. 16

Since the message of the Gospel remains the same from the days of the early church, neither has the world changed in its opposition to the core of our faith. The apostles of the book of Acts exemplify the uncompromised proclamation of the Gospel in the face of adversity. This boldness sparked a mass multiplication of believers since they did not allow the world around them to intimidate them.

The writer would like to share the following excerpt on Dr. T. L. Osborn's *Legacy of Faith*, which are his shared secrets of success throughout his ministry as it also continues under the direction of his daughter and successor, Dr. LaDonna Osborn. The author of this book highly regards this ministry in their wisdom to continue in the message of redemption in their ongoing seventy plus years of ministry throughout the world. We need to glean and learn from such role models as these:

> There is no magic in the concepts that Dr. Osborn teaches. They are strategic, dynamic, pragmatic and biblical. When he says 'biblical,' he means that they are rooted in the redemptive work of Christ. More than one concept has gotten off-course; such as healing, the gifts of the Spirit, church structure or leadership, or so-called spiritual warfare and intercessory prayer. They have gotten off-course because they have been rooted in ideology-doctrine or belief-that is not accountable to the redemptive work of Christ.
>
> Dr. Osborn teaches that Good News is 'The Message that Works.' He attributes the long success of his global ministry to the teaching of this message. The message is simple, but fundamental. Through this message, people are acquainted with: 1) Their origin in God, 2) Satan's deception, 3) Christ's death and resurrection, and what that means, and 4) the reality of his life in believers today. Who was Jesus? What did He do? Why did He do it? Whom did He do it for? Those are

the essentials. And as Christians grow in truth, they should re-visit everything they believe in light of this, which is the essence of God's plan for man.[122]

The Example of John the Baptist

John 1:19–30 can be carefully observed as we look into the example of John the Baptist's conviction regarding his ministry. First of all, the priests and Levites were sent from Jerusalem to ask John about who he was. As we read his response, we can presume that he knew what they were really asking: Was he the Messiah? Was he the anointed one?

In his humility and discernment, he perceived their intentions and would not attribute any glory to himself for the ministry to which he was called. Nor did he attempt to validate himself regarding his authorization. He simply stated his mandate "to make straight the way of the Lord" (vs.23, NKJV).

Yet still, they questioned his authorization for ministry. He intelligently brings them back into focus in regard to who his ministry was about. "After me comes a Man who is preferred before me, for He was before me" (vs.30, NKJV). Simply stated, Jesus is the one who is preferred. We are to direct the attention of those we minister onto Jesus who is the Redeemer since no one can be saved, except through faith in his name.

With this in mind, as we glean from John's example, we are challenged to live by the same conviction. The attitude we take on as believers in Christ is not to prefer our reputation above the pre-eminence of Christ. We will always face the challenge to hold the integrity of humility by not allowing others to attribute to us any such glory when they distinguish our natural birth identity as though it was the source of spiritual authority.

---

[122] Osborn, T. L. *Legacy of Faith Collection—Pioneer of Mass Evangelism.* Copyright 2011 by Osborn Ministries International. Publisher: Harrison House Publishers, Tulsa, OK. 74153, pp. 329–330

Paul the apostle wrote, "Not that we are sufficient of ourselves to think of anything as being from ourselves, but our sufficiency is from God, who also made us sufficient ministers of the new covenant" (2 Corinthians 3:5–4a, NKJV). In another epistle, Paul exhorted the Colossians "that in all things He may have the preeminence" (1:18). Christ is to have first place.

Jesus also declared, "And I, if I am lifted up from the earth, will draw all peoples to Myself" (John 12:32, NKJV). For any steward of the Gospel who draws attention to themselves is to cast a shadow in the view of the glorious light who is to shine in the hearts of all. Let us endeavor to live by the same conviction as that of John the Baptist.

If we are to truly understand our spiritual position in the kingdom of heaven, we must never be moved away from the essential truth that "ye must be born again." In Christ, we are citizens of heaven. Being born again is not a mere terminology or title, but rather, it is a crucial part to being accepted into the kingdom of heaven. This brings to focus our God-given identity as believers.

Since this is so, as believers, no one is able to place faith in their natural birth identity, thinking these attributes "extra" spiritual authority gaining us special position, rights, and privileges. These faculties of the natural birth are not substantial for effective ministry as we reach out to this world. To do so is to place these limits toward other believers in Christ in their going forth to minister across cultural boundaries.

How vital it is that we need to remain confident in who we are in Christ. We are not to exhibit partiality among one another due our natural birth. We must always remember these words of Paul:

> There is neither Jew nor Greek, there is neither slave nor free, there is neither male nor female; for you are all one in Christ Jesus (Galatians 3:28, NKJV).

While we appreciate the uniqueness of our ethnicities and personalities, we must recognize that any ministry which God raises up is not due to their racial or tribal distinction, status, age, or gender.

When we do this, we take away from the centrality of Christ who dwells within each person. When individual's come forth in the ministry that God has given, it is because they have decided to follow Jesus as they pursue the higher call of God in Christ Jesus. They have caught the heart of God to reach the lost. They have heard his call to go into all the world and preach the Gospel. God will honor the faith and obedience of the faithful and obedient follower of Christ.

What Is the Conclusion of the Matter?

It is time to get back to the uncompromised simple message of the Gospel of Jesus Christ. Upon hearing numerous reports in many nations across the world where the Gospel has spread like wildfire, causing great impact, one begins to wonder: What has been missing for my people all along over the last several decades? The Gospel, uncompromised, will bring the same kind of impact among Indigenous communities as in any other place in the world. We must realize that the Gospel is not a racial, tribal, gender, or status, or a "gatekeeper's" Gospel.

Our focus in Christian ministry ought to be to properly teach the truths of redemption in matters pertaining to our original design that God intended that all of mankind were to be made in his image. Through Christ in us, we are transformed in his image. Christ came to restore to every individual their true spiritual identity. When we walk in the revelation of our restored spiritual identity in Christ, we no longer sense the need to identify with the things of this world for significance, including the culture in which we were born. Instead, we come to realize that our true significance, identity, and dignity has been restored through the work of Christ.

As we conclude, it is the unadulterated message of the Gospel that will bring forth restoration and healing of broken lives, which have been tainted by sin. The key issue in redemption regards the birth that counts, a spiritual birth, being born again through faith in Christ. When this transpires in the lives of people is when communities begin to transform from glory to glory. For it is only the truth of the Gospel that will cause complicated issues to resolve, and lives will improve while true reconciliation, healing, equality, and unity becomes proficient within that redeemed community.

When received, the truths of the Gospel of redemption hold the ability to eradicate strongholds of inequality and discrimination, segregation, and separation in all its forms. When the writer continues to hear the reports of the widespread impact which the Gospel has made in many and various dark places of the world, the writer is inspired to rise to the challenge and has no doubt in her mind that this is the only answer for her people, including all the nations of the world. The author will close with these words of Paul:

> For I am not ashamed of the Gospel of Christ, for it the power of God unto salvation for everyone who believers, for the Jew first and also for the Greek. For in it the righteousness of God is revealed from faith to faith; as it is written, the just shall live by faith. (Romans 1:16–17, NKJV)

APPENDIX A

Jarvis J. Williams and Octavio Javier Esqueda share these thought-provoking words in the following two articles:

Though all have sinned (Rom. 3:23), God has acted to unify all things and all people in Christ (Eph. 1:9–3:10), who died for our sins to deliver sinners from this present evil age (Gal. 1:4). Racism is part of this evil age. By faith in Christ, Jesus's blood and resurrection reconcile a diversity of humans into one transformed and ethnically and racially diverse Christian community (1 Pet. 2:9; Rev. 5:9).

Thus, all kinds of racially and ethnically diverse people can be justified by faith in Christ (Rom. 3:21–4:25); repent of and turn from their sins (Acts 2:1–38); and be reconciled to God (Rom. 5:6–10) and to each other (Eph. 2:11–22).

Throughout Scripture, we see that the gospel demands this diverse community intentionally to pursue one another in love (John 13:34–35; 1 John 2:10; 3:10-11,14,16,18,23; 4:7–12,20–21)… Churches need a robust understanding of the old gospel and how it demands us to pursue racial harmony. We also need an informed understanding of race, racism, and white supremacy and the intentional and unintentional ways in which they work in our churches and in society. Then, our churches need to create specific goals and a plan by which to pursue racial harmony in our churches and communities.[123]

---

[123] Williams, Jarvis J. "A Gospel that's Big Enough to Heal the Racial Divide." August 21, 2017. Theology and Spirituality, Christianity Today, http://www.

Jesus was also an immigrant in his own land. He was from Nazareth and when he ministered in Judea he suffered discrimination from his own countrymen. At the beginning of his ministry, Nathanael expressed these words that reflected the common perception of those who believed some people were better than others because of the region where they lived, "Nazareth! Can anything good come from there?" (John 1:46).

Nazareth was a town in the northern region of Galilee and that was regarded as less important than Judea, in the south where the capital city, Jerusalem, was located. Unfortunately, as human beings, we have the tendency to become regionalists and to value our own land over others. Jesus, the King of Kings and Lord of Lords, identifies himself with those who are marginalized and whose value is downplayed because of their birthplace. Just Like Jesus—All Christians are immigrants. The Bible clearly teaches that when we receive the gift of eternal life that Jesus graciously offers, we become citizens of heaven and now live as foreigners and strangers on earth as the people of faith. (Heb. 11:13) Our faith reminds us that this life is not all that exists and that now in Christ we have a new heavenly citizenship that unites all believers (Phil. 3:20). This reality does not invalidate our national citizenship nor prevents us from actively serving our society, but it does give us a broader, eternal perspective.[124]

---

christiantytoday.org

[124] Esqueda, Octavio Javier. "What's Your Immigration Status? Divine." Jesus was an immigrant and taught his followers to welcome and care for foreigners. Octavio Javier Esqueda. September 6, 2017, *Theology and Spirituality*, Christianity Today, http://www.christianitytoday.org

Appendix B

D r. LaDonna Osborn's helpful and thought-provoking obser-
vation from her book, Cross-Cultural Communications in a
Multicultural Church (it was difficult to select which parts to leave
out, however, since this flows so well, the writer felt it necessary to
include the whole as it gives the reader much to consider):

Recognizing diversity as a fact in the American culture challenges the church to formulate methodology that transmits the
Christian faith across ethnic barriers, while respecting the uniqueness
of various groups.

Consider three of the most obvious options that are available to
the church, segregation, integration, and participation.

Historically, segregation of ethnic groups in America has not
served the best interest of society as a whole or of specific groups
individually. Ultimately, segregation engenders division, and division
is contrary to the goal of the Christian message. The principle of
spiritual unity is included in Jesus's prayer recorded in the Gospel
of John: "And now I am no longer in the world, but they are in the
world, and I am coming to you. Holy Father, protect them in your
name that you have given me, so that they may be on, as we are one."

The principle of unity was advocated by the Apostle Paul in
his first letter to the Corinthians: 'Now I appeal to you, brothers
and sisters, by the name of our Lord Jesus Christ, that all of you be
in agreement and there be no divisions among you, but that you be
united in the same mind and same purposes.' While it is not the purpose of this author to present a detailed historical argument against
segregation, it can be generally agreed that historical evidence sup-

ports the claim that segregation did not serve the public good in America, and the Christian scriptures suggest a higher ideal for the human creation.

Integration of the various ethnic groups into one single group is a second option available to the church. While this appears to fulfill the ideal of social unity, the historic record again testifies to the failure of this option. Integration results in the loss of the individual distinction of all groups except for that of the dominant group. The dominant culture, of the majority, in America is Caucasian. As the population mix continues to change, it is important to know that the term "majority" does not refer to population numbers, but to the group holding the reins of power. In America, the majority of economic and political power is still in the hands of the Caucasian, middle class male. Author Anne Wilson Shaef refers to American society as the White Male System or "the reality" by which all other groups are assessed. Radical or ethnic groups, other than Caucasian, are classified as "minority" regardless of their numeric strength. It is the opinion of this author that while segregation engenders division, integration results in domination of the weaker by the more powerful. What we must remember the value set forth in Christian scripture: 'there is no longer Jew or Greek, there is no longer slave or free, there is no longer male and female; for all of you are one in Christ Jesus.' The biblical principle of equality between all people regardless of race, economic status, gender (or other distinctions) establishes a criterion by which Christian ministries must be evaluated.

The third option available to the church is participation. While segregation engenders division and integration results in domination, it is the premise of this author that participation promotes restoration. Restoration of the relationship between God and the creation is the central theme of the Christian society. While there are myriad theological views, it can generally be agreed that this restoration involves participation between God and the creation: initiative on the part of God (grace) and response on the part of the human persons (faith). This principle of participation is seen throughout the biblical text, and directly stated in the Gospel of John: 'For God so loved the world that he gave his only Son, so that everyone who believes in him may not perish but may have eternal life.'

When considering the options available to the church in a multicultural society, we must remember the example of Jesus's ministry that also occurred in a cross-cultural setting. his example suggest that the church today needs to develop cross-cultural communication and participation skills.[125]

[125] Osborn, LaDonna C. *Cross-Cultural Communications in a Multicultural Church.* Copyright 2002, Publisher: Osborn Publishers, Tulsa, OK. 74102 USA, pp. 12–16.

Appendix C

I n his book, *The Father and His Family*, E. W. Kenyon writes:

Paul writes in 1 Timothy 3:15, 'that thou mayest know how men ought to behave themselves in the House of God, which is the church of the Living God, the pillar ground, (or stay) of the truth.'

'How we ought to behave ourselves,' not in a Church building when we come together for services or fellowship, but in the Family, the Household of God; that may mean in your work, or in your pleasures; it may mean in the Assembly of the Family. Paul is writing to tell us how we ought to act toward the Brethren, toward the Sisters, toward the young and aged, in this wonderful Household of Faith, this Family of God.[126]

In his book, *What Happened from the Throne to the Cross*, E. W. Kenyon also writes:

The Abrahamic Covenant gave to Israel its home, Palestine. It gave them what was known as the Mosaic Law, the Priesthood, the atonement, the sacrifices. These all had been annulled when Jesus said, 'It is finished', on the cross, and the veil of the temple had been rent from top to bottom. God shows by that act, that the Covenant was ended and that the New Covenant, that Jesus had spoken of, was

---

[126] Kenyon, E. W. *The Father and His Family*. Twenty-Sixth Printing. Copyright 2013. Publisher: Kenyon's Gospel Publishing Society, Lynwood, Washington, USA, pg. 184

to come into being at once. The Old Covenant had been with natural man. This New Covenant is to have a New Creation Man. The other Covenant had servants. This Covenant had sons. Ephesians 2:10 'For we are his workmanship, created in Christ Jesus for good works, which God afore prepared that we should walk in them.' 2 Cor. 5:17 'Wherefore if any man is in Christ, he is a new creature: the old things are passed away; behold they are become new. But all these things are of God.'

This is the new type of humanity. God has given them his own nature, eternal life, thus it was the beginning of man with eternal life, the nature of God. There is no doubt but what he could have had this nature in the Garden of Eden if he had eaten of the tree of life instead of the tree of the knowledge of good and evil. It was the beginning of the Family of God.[127]

---

[127] Kenyon, E. W. *What Happened from the Cross to the Throne.* Twenty-Sixth Printing. Copyright 2010. Publisher: Kenyon's Gospel Publishing Society, Lynwood, WA. USA, pg. 142

Appendix D

I n his book, *New Creation Realities*, E. W. Kenyon wrote:

Our redemption is from the dominion of Satan, and when Christ arose from the dead and presented his own blood before the Supreme Court of the Universe, and it was accepted our Redemption was a settled thing. Then He sat down at the right of the Majesty on High. When He sat down, Satan had been defeated.

Everything that justice had demanded had been accomplished. Now God has, a legal right to give man Eternal Life, but He had no right to give man Eternal Life until there had been a perfect redemption. So, Rom. 3:21-26 is the Holy Spirit's exposition of this blessed Reality. 'But now apart from the law a righteousness of God hath been unveiled, being witnessed by the law and the prophets.'[128]

You understand that man's basic need was Righteousness, the ability to stand in the Father's presence without the sense of guilt or inferiority, and so He declares that God has unveiled a new source of Righteousness, and that source of Righteousness is witnessed by the law and the prophets, 'even the righteousness of God on the ground of faith in Jesus Christ.' And the strange thing is it is based upon

---

[128] Kenyon, E. W. *New Creation Realities*. Twenty-Seventh Printing. Copyright 2011. Kenyon's Gospel Publishing Society, Lynwood, WA. 98046-0973, pg. 46

simple faith in Jesus, or in acting upon what God has said in regard to his Son.[129]

In his book, *The Bible in the Light of Our Redemption*, E. W. Kenyon wrote:

The Father-God looks upon the New Creation as He looks upon Christ. The new man does not belong to the world and has no more part in his relation to Satan that Christ had. John 17:6, 'They are not of the world even as I am not of the world.' The Father-God loves the new man even as He loves Christ. John 17:23, 'That the world may know that Thou didst send me and lovest them even a Thou lovest me.' The Father hears the requests of the New Creation even as He heard Christ because that one prays in the name of Jesus. This new man can bring the Omnipotent Creator to action on his behalf by using the authority of the Name of Jesus. John 16:23-24, 'Verily, verily I say unto you, if ye shall ask anything of the Father, he will give it you in My name.' How limitless in power and authority is the life of the one who has been made a New Creation in him![130]

The Father-God looks upon the New Creation as He looks upon Christ. The new man does not belong to the world and has no more part in his relation to Satan that Christ had. John 17:6, 'They are not of the world even as I am not of the world.' The Father-God loves the new man even as He loves Christ. John 17:23, 'That the world may know that Thou didst send me and lovest them even a Thou lovest me.' The Father hears the requests of the New Creation even as He heard Christ because that one prays in the name of Jesus. This new man can bring the Omnipotent Creator to action on his behalf by using the authority of the Name of Jesus. John 16:23-24,

---

[129] Kenyon, E. W. *New Creation Realities*. Twenty-Seventh Printing. Copyright 2011. Kenyon's Gospel Publishing Society, Lynwood, WA. 98046-0973, pg. 46
[130] Kenyon, E. W. *The Bible in Light of Our Redemption*. Twenty-Eighth Printing. Copyright 2011. Kenyon's Gospel Publishing Society, Lynwood, WA. 98046-0973, pg. 183

'Verily, verily I say unto you, if ye shall ask anything of the Father, he will give it you in My name.' How limitless in power and authority is the life of the one who has been made a New Creation in him![131]

---

[131] Kenyon, E. W. *The Bible in Light of Our Redemption*. Twenty-Eighth Printing. Copyright 2011. Kenyon's Gospel Publishing Society, Lynwood, WA. 98046-0973, pg. 183

Appendix E

In her book, *Jesus & Women*, Daisy Washburn Osborn offers readers these empowering words:

You have a purpose that is higher than activity or secular profession. You have a purpose that is higher than any social level. You have a purpose that began before the foundation of the world when God said to himself, 'Let's make people' (Genesis 1:26). You were in God's mind then, and he had a plan for you that He has never abandoned. All of hell and every demon power cannot rob God of his purpose in you, because you are his creation, made for his glory in the earth. That purpose will cause you to wake up in the morning and say with Paul, 'It is no longer I who live, but Christ lives in me; and the life which I now lie in the flesh I live by faith in the Son of God who loved me and gave Himself for me' (Galatians 2:20). You are the body of Christ in the earth. You are the holy place of his habitation. You are the tabernacle of his anointing. You are the dispenser of his mercy and his grace in this earth. You are the light of the world. You are the salt of the earth. You are the preservation. You are the healer. You are the forgiver. You are the tabernacle that fulfills God's awesome purpose in the earth today.[132]

---

[132] Osborn, Daisy Washburn. *Jesus & Women*. Copyright 2000 by LaDonna C. Osborn. Publisher: Osborn Publishers, Tulsa, OK. 74102, pg. 44

APPENDIX F

E xecutive Director of the Billy Graham Center, Ed Stetzer, shares these noteworthy words:

We need a reemphasis on Gospel clarity. Being labeled Christian no longer means a 'social Christian,' but instead is someone who's been changed by the power of the gospel, if indeed you have. This is a vital theological shift in the way we are viewed and should view our land. Understanding these shifts is necessary in part because we live in an age of outrage. People in our land get ticked off over things that they don't like. This calls us to Gospel clarity. And missionary identity, seeing ourselves as strangers and temporary residents, is what will pull us toward showing and sharing the love of Jesus as we should.

We Are a Convictional Minority

At one time, we were perceived (incorrectly, I think) as a religious majority. Today, we're a convictional minority. This is key because when you're a convictional minority, you don't fit in the mainstream of culture. We are statistically a minority of people in our culture who think differently than the mainstream culture. We are not walking around thinking, We're the majority. You're going to do what I say.

You're going to accept all my standards.

A lot of people still think Christendom when they think American, Canadian, British, or whatever. They believe they need to take back the country because it's theirs and others are interlopers. The reality is, we are the interlopers. We are the strangers and foreigners. When we think like a convictional minority, we'll engage culture less with "You owe me" and more with "How can I engage you the culture we are in via the mission we are on?[133]

---

[133] https://www.christianitytoday.com/edstetser/2018/july/missionary-identity.html

APPENDIX G

Reconciliation Ministries Network published the following article which sheds light on this important exercise:

A Biblical Theology of Missions

The barrier to sharing the Gospel with non-Jews took extraordinary measures to overcome, including angelic visitation, visions, and providential timing (Acts 10:3, 11, 19-20). Most cultures tend toward ethnocentrism, toward a prejudicial preference of their own culture to all others. Ethnocentrism is prejudicial because the strengths of other cultures are often not appreciated. The attitude that "we are the people" prevails. This pride is perhaps strongest among those who have the least experience with other cultures.

Worldview:

Culture may be defined as the particular solutions to the needs of life adopted by a group of people. It rests upon beliefs. The deepest beliefs and assumptions about the world, including values, perspectives, taboos and behaviors, constitute one's worldview. A worldview constitutes a cognitive grid through which perceptions are interpreted. Typically, this worldview cannot be articulated by the holder, since it is taken for granted, and is so deeply ingrained from birth. A person wearing glasses, for instance, doesn't notice the lenses, yet they are unique to the needs of the wearer, and would not help most others to properly see.

Networking:

"Two are better than one, because they have a good return for their work." (Eccles. 4:9). Jesus sent out the 12 and the 70 by two's (Mark 6:7; Luke 10:1). Two not only lightens the load, but makes the load light (Matt. 11:28-30). Additionally, since Christians specialize in ministry, we need to both assist other Christians in their ministry and call upon them to assist us in ministry to others (see The Urban Christian, by Ray Bakke, InterVarsity Press).[134]

In keeping with cross-cultural ministry, Karl Dahlfred's article also briefs these insightful observations about the Apostle Paul's approach in his successful ministry while crossing cultural barriers as they were bridged with message of the Gospel:

Although free from the requirement of keeping the ceremonial law, and free from the penalty of failing to keep the law of God perfectly, and certainly free from the burdensome rabbinic superstructure of rules built around the law, he still very much regarded himself as under the authority of God expressed in his word.

Scripture, in its theology, worldview, commands and principles, set the boundaries for his adaptation to the people he was trying to reach.

The same must apply to us. Every human culture reflects common grace, but every culture also reflects the fall. We must not adapt to that which contradicts Scripture.

Paul's understanding of this principle becomes clear when the entirety of his writings are examined. He refused to accommodate to the "wisdom" of the popular Hellenistic worldview around him, because he realized that it negated the gospel at its very heart, however sophisticated it might have sounded. Indeed, Paul never con-

---

[134] RMNi—Reconciliation Ministries Network. "Introduction of Cross-Cultural Ministry," Copyright1998–2017byReconciliationMinistriesNetworkInc,https://www.rmni.org/teaching-resources/articles/cross-cultural-ministry/introduction-cross-cultural.html

doned diversity or accommodation in matters of doctrine. He did not accommodate the seedy practices of contemporary itinerate teachers. He most certainly did not accommodate the "acceptable" immorality of Corinthian society. Human culture and human tradition are negotiable. God's Word is not, ever.

Contextualization, then, is both unavoidable and good. The gospel can, and should, transform people in every culture. And we must identify with those we are trying to reach and adapt to their culture, no matter what discomfort it causes us. However, the gospel also challenges and condemns every culture at some points (including our own). Where the Bible draws a line, we must draw a line.

The point of contextualization is not comfort, but clarity. The gospel will never be completely comfortable in any fallen society or to any sinful human being. Our goal is to make sure that we do not put any obstacles in the way of the gospel, and that the only stumbling block is the stumbling block of the cross itself. (© 9Marks. Website: www.9Marks.org. Email: info@9marks.org. Toll Free: (888) 543-1030.)"[135]

---

[135] Dahlfred, Karl. "Paul's Principles for Cross-Cultural Ministry." July 11th, 2009, https://www.dahlfred.com/en/prayer-letters/231-pauls-principles-for-cross-cultural-ministry

BIBLIOGRAPHY

Articles

Dahlfred, Karl. "Paul's Principles for Cross Cultural Ministry" July 11, 2009.
https://www.dahlfred.com/en/prayer-letters/231-pauls-principles-for-cross-cultural-ministry

Esqueda, Octavio Javier. "What's Your Immigration Status." September 6, 2017.
http://www.chrisitanitytoday.org

Mennonite Central Committee. "Vision and Mission"
http://mcccanada.ca/learn/about/mission

Padgett, Alan G. "What is Biblical Equality?" Website What is biblical Equality—Padgett.pdf.
www.biblicalequality.org/index.php?option+com_docman&task=doc_download

Purse, Samaritan's "About Us." https://www.samaritanspurse.org/our-ministry/about-us

RMNi—Reconciliation Ministries Network. "Introduction of Cross-Cultural Ministry," Copyright ©1998–2017 by Reconciliation Ministries Network Inc. https://www.rmni.org/teaching-resources/articles/cross-cultural-ministry/introduction-cross-cultural.html

Shin, Sarah, "Racial Difference Without Division, The Power of an Ethnicity-Honoring Witness." Christianity Today. November 14, 2017, http://www.christianitytoday.org

Smith, Efram, "Pastors: God Calls Us to Cross-Cultural Ministry." https://sojo.net/articles/pastors-god-calls-us-cross-cultural-ministry

Stetzer, Ed. "Missionary Identity." https://www.christianitytoday.com/edstetser/2018/july/missionary-identity.html

Williams, Jarvis J. "A Gospel that's Big Enough to Heal the Racial Divide by Jarvis J. Williams. "How Christians Can Combat Racism Theologically After Charlottesville—A Pair of Scholars Bring Up a New and Old Approach." Clifton Clarke and Jarvis J. Williams, August 21, 2017, http://www.christianitytoday.org

Bible Translations

Amplified Classic. Copyright 1998–2017 Olive Tree Bible Software

English Standard Version. Copyright 1998-2017 Olive Tree Bible Software

Holman Christian Standard Bible. Copyright 1998-2017 Olive Tree Bible Software

King James Version. Copyright 1998–2017 Olive Tree Bible Software

Living Bible, The. Copyright 1998–2017 Olive Tree Bible Software

New English Translation. Copyright 1998–2017 Olive Tree Bible Software

New International Version. Copyright 1998–2017 Olive Tree Bible Software

Commentaries and Dictionaries

2003, 2005, 2010, Oxford University Press, Great Clarendon Street, Oxford

Lecture Notes

Christian, Shelley, "Spirit, Soul, and Body Wholeness," Seminar notes at NTOMI Discipleship Bible School, Ft. Providence, NT, November 18-11, 2013

Books

Anderson, Neil T. *Victory Over Darkness.* E-book Edition originally created 2013, Copyright 1990 by Regal Books (First Edition), 2000 by Neil T. Anderson (Second Edition), 2013 by Neil T. Anderson (Third Edition), Publisher: Bethany House Publishers, Bloomington, MN. 55438

Brown, Marie. *Equal Redemption for All.* Copyright 1990, by H. Marie Brown, Publisher: Marie Brown Ministries, Tulsa, OK. 74170

Brown, Marie. *God Has No Favorites.* Copyright 2001 by H. Marie Brown, Publisher: Marie Brown Ministries, Inc. Tulsa, OK. 74170

Brown, Marie. *Possessing Your Inheritance—Living in Your Righteousness.* Copyright 2007 by H. Marie Brown, Publisher: Marie Brown Ministries, Inc. Tulsa, OK. 74170

Brown, Marie. *The Unstoppable Church.* Copyright 2010 by H. Marie Brown, Publisher: Marie Brown Ministries Inc., Columbia, SC. 29260, USA

Capps, Charles. *Your Spiritual Authority: Learn to Use Your God-given Rights to Live in Victory.* Copyright 1980, 1982 by Charles

Capps, Revised Copyright 1994, Publisher: Capps Publishing, England AK 72046, E-book edition

Chambers, Oswald. *Conformed to His Image—The Servant as His Lord, Lessons on Living Like Jesus.* Copyright 1995 Oswald Chambers Publications Association Limited, Publisher: Discovery House Publishers, Grand Rapids, MI. 49501

Copeland, Kenneth. *Now We Are in Christ Jesus.* Copyright 1980, Eagle Mountain International Church, Incorporated, a.k.a. Kenneth Copeland Ministries. Publisher: Kenneth Copeland Publications, Fort Worth, TX. 76192-0001

Copeland, Kenneth. *Racism in the Church—Kill the Root, Destroy the Tree.* E-book Edition. Copyright 2016 by Kenneth Copeland. Published in Partnership with: Harrison House Publishers, Tulsa, OK. 74145 and Kenneth Copeland Publications, Fort Worth, TX. 76192-0001

Cromwell, Michael. *A Biblical Approach to Racism.* Copyright 1999, Publisher: Xlibris Corporation, www.Xlibris.com

Cross, John R. *By This Name.* Copyright 2010 by GoodSeed International, Publisher: GoodSeed International, Olds, Alberta, Canada

Cross, John R. *The Stranger on the Road to Emmaus.* Edition 5a. Copyright 2014, Publisher: GoodSeed International, Olds AB, T4H 1P5

Hagin, Kenneth E. *Paul's Revelation.* Electronic Edition. Published 2013, Copyright 1983, Publisher: Rhema Bible Church, a.k.a. Kenneth Hagin Ministries, Inc. USA

Hagin, Kenneth E. *The Believer's Authority.* The Believer's Authority, Legacy Edition. Copyright 1967, 1986, 2004, 2009. Rhema Bible Church, Electronic Edition

Hagin, Kenneth E. *The Name of Jesus.* Legacy Edition. Copyright 1979, 2006, 2007 Rhema Bible Church Electronic Edition. Published 2010, a.k.a. Kenneth Hagin Ministries, Inc.

Hagin, Kenneth E. *The New Birth.* Electronic Edition. Copyright 1975 Rhema Bible Church, a.k.a. Kenneth Hagin Ministries, Inc. All rights reserved. Printed in USA

Hagin, Kenneth E. *The Triumphant Church.* Copyright 1993 Rhema Bible Church, Electronic Edition. Published 2010, a.k.a. Kenneth Hagin Ministries, Inc.

Hagin, Kenneth E. *Understanding the Anointing.* Copyright 1983 Rhema Bible Church, Electronic Edition. Published 2013, a.k.a. Kenneth Hagin Ministries, Inc.

Ham, Ken, A., Charles Ware. *One Race One Blood.* First Printing October 2010. Copyright 2007 by Master Books. Publisher: Master Books, Green Forest, AZ. (Kindle Locations 1263-1265). Master Books

Hull, Gretchen Gaebelein, *Equal to Serve.* Copyright by Gretchen Gaebelein Hull. Publisher: Baker Books, 1998, Grand Rapids, MI. 49516-6287

Hyatt, Susan C. *In the Spirit, We're Equal.* Copyright 1998 by Hyatt International Ministries, Inc. Publisher: Hyatt International Ministries, Inc. Dallas, Texas.

Jones, Stanley E. *The Christ of the Mount—A Living Exposition of Jesus' Words as the Only Practical Way of Life.* Festival Edition. Published 1981, Copyright 1931, Copyright renewal 1958 by E. Stanley Jones. Publisher: Festival Books, Abingdon Nashville, TN.

Jones, Stanley E. *The Reconstruction of the Church—On What Pattern?*"
Copyright 1970 by Abingdon Press. Publisher: Abingdon Press,
Nashville, TN.

Jones, E. Stanley. *The Unshakeable Kingdom.* Copyright 1972 by
Abingdon Press. Publisher: McNett Press, Bellingham, WA.
98277

Johnson, David and VanVonderen, Jeff. *The Subtle Power of Spiritual
Abuse.* Copyright 1991. E-book Edition 2011, Publisher:
Bethany House Publishers, 11400 Hampshire Ave South,
Bloomington, Minnesota, 55438, www.bethanyhouse.com

Joyner, Rick. *Overcoming Racism.* Copyright 1996, E-book Edition
2010, Publisher: MorningStar Publications a Division of
MorningStar Fellowship Church, Fort Mill, SC. 29715 www.
MoringStarMinistries.org. "Part I—Racism and the Spirit of
Death"

Kenyon, E. W. *New Creation Realities.* Twenty-Seventh Printing.
Copyright 2011. Kenyon's Gospel Publishing Society, Lynwood,
WA. 98046-0973

Kenyon, E. W. *Identification—A Romance in Redemption.* Twenty-
Sixth Printing. Copyright 2012 by Kenyon's Gospel Publishing
Society. Publisher: Kenyon's Gospel Publishing Society,
Lynwood, WA. 98046-0973

Kenyon, E. W. *The Bible in the Light of Our Redemption.* Twenty-
Eighth Printing, Copyright 2011 by Kenyon's Gospel Publishing
Society. Printed in USA, pp 26–30

Kenyon, E. W. The Father and His Family. Twenty-Sixth Printing,
Copyright 2013. Publisher: Kenyon's Gospel Publishing Society,
Lynwood, Washington, USA

Kenyon, E. W. *The Hidden Man—An Unveiling of the Subconscious Mind.* Copyright 2012. Twenty-Fourth Printing. Publisher: Kenyon's Gospel Publishing Services Inc, Lynnwood, Washington

Kenyon, E. W. *The New Kind of Love.* Twenty-First Printing. Copyright 2000 by Kenyon's Gospel Publishing Society. Publisher: Kenyon's Gospel Publishing Society, Lynwood, WA. 98046-0973

Kenyon, E. W. *Two Kinds of Righteousness—The Most Important Message Ever Offered to the Church.* Copyright 2011, Twenty-Fifth Printing, Kenyon's Gospel Publishing Society, Inc. Lynwood, WA. 98046-0973

Kenyon, E. W. *What Happened from the Cross to the Throne.* Twenty-Sixth Printing, Copyright 2010. Publisher: Kenyon's Gospel Publishing Society, Lynwood, WA. USA

Kenyon, E. W., *What We Are in Christ.* Second Printing. Copyright 2013 by Kenyon's Gospel Publishing Society. Publisher: Kenyon's Gospel Publishing Society, Lynwood, WA. 98046-0973

Lindsay, Freda. *The Second Wind.* Copyright 1999. Christ for the Nations. Publisher: Christ for the Nations, Dallas, TX. 75376-9000

McIntosh & Twyman, Drs. *The Archko Volume.* Translated by Dr.'s. McIntosh & Twyman of the Antiquarian Lodge, Genoa, Italy, Unabridged Edition. Copyright 1975 by Keats Publishing, Inc. Keats Publishing, Inc., 212 Elm Street, New Canaan, Connecticut 06840 USA

Nee, Watchman. *Sit, Walk, Stand—The Process of Christian Maturity.* Copyright 2009 by CLC Ministries International. Publishers: CLC Publications, Fort Washington, PA. 19034

Nee, Watchman. *Spiritual Authority*. Electronic Edition. Copyright 2014. Publisher: Christian Fellowship Publisher, Inc. New York, NY.

Osborn, Daisy Washburn. *Five Choices for Women Who Win*. Copyright 2004 by LaDonna C. Osborn. Publisher: Osborn Ministries Intl., Tulsa, OK. 74102

Osborn, Daisy Washburn. *Jesus & Women*. Copyright 2000 by LaDonna C. Osborn. Publisher: Osborn Publishers, Tulsa, OK. 74102

Osborn, Daisy Washburn. *The Woman Believer*. Copyright 1990. Publisher: OSFO Publishers, Tulsa, OK. 74102, USA

Osborn, Daisy Wasburn. *Women & Self Esteem*. Copyright 2008 by LaDonna C. Osborn. Publisher: Osborn Ministries Intl. Tulsa, OK. 74102

Osborn, LaDonna C. *Cross-Cultural Communications in a Multicultural Church*. Copyright 2002. Publisher: Osborn Publishers, Tulsa OK. 74102 USA, pp. 12–16.

Osborn, LaDonna C. *God's Big Picture*. Copyright 2001 by LaDonna C. Osborn. Publisher: Osborn Publishers, Tulsa OK. 74102

Osborn, T. L. *God's Love Plan*. Copyright 1984. Publisher: OSFO BOOKS, OSFO INTERNATIONAL, Osborn Publishers, Tulsa, OK. 74102, USA

Osborn, T. L. *How to Be Born Again*. Copyright 2002 by LaDonna C. Osborn. Publishers: Osborn Publishers, Tulsa, OK. 74102

Osborn, T. L. *Legacy of Faith Collection—Pioneer of Mass Evangelism*. Copyright 2011 by Osborn Ministries International. Publisher: Harrison House Publishers, Tulsa OK. 74153, pp. 329–330

Osborn, T. L. *The Message that Works.* Copyright 2004 by LaDonna C. Osborn. Publisher: Osborn Publishers, Tulsa OK. 74102

Osborn, T. L. *You Are God's Best.* Copyright 2013 by LaDonna C. Osborn. Publishers: Osborn Ministries International, Tulsa, OK. 74102

Platt, David. *A Compassionate Call to Counter Culture in a World of Racism.* Copyright 2015 by David Platt. Publisher: Tyndale House of Publisher, Inc. www.tyndale.com

Platt, David. *A Compassionate Call to Counter Culture in a World of Unreached People Groups.* Electronic Edition, Copyright 2015 by David Platt. Publisher, Tyndale House Publishers, Inc. USA, A Call To Counter Culture

Smith, Craig. *The White Man's Gospel.* Copyright 1997. Publisher: Indian Life Books, A Division of Indian Life Ministries, P.O. Box 3765, RPO Redwood Center, Winnipeg, Manitoba R2W 3R6

Smith, Malcom. *The Lost Secret of the New Covenant.* Copyright 2002. Publisher: Harrison House, Inc. Tulsa, Oklahoma, 74153

Renner, Rick. *Dressed to Kill—A Biblical Approach to Spiritual Warfare and Armor.* Copyright 1991 by Rick Renner. Paperback Edition 2014, Third Printing, Publisher: Harrison House, Tulsa, OK. 74145

Renner, Rick. *Merchandising the Anointing—Developing Discernment for These Last Days.* Copyright 1990 by Rick Renner Ministries. Publisher: Albury Publishing, Tulsa, OK. 74147-0406

Renner, Rick. *Seducing Spirits and Doctrines of Demons.* Copyright 1998 by Rick Renner Ministries. Publisher: Albury Publishing, Tulsa, OK. 74147-0406

Varner, Kelley. *The Three Prejudices.* Copyright 1997. Destiny Image Publishers, Inc. Shippensburg, PA. 1997

Yohannon, K. P. *Against the Wind—Finishing Well in a World of Compromise.* Copyright 2004. Publisher: GFA Books, a Division of Gospel for Asia, 1800 Golden Trail Court, Carrollton, TX. 7501

Interviews

(All interviews held confidential; the names of the interviewees are withheld by mutual agreement)
Interview by Author White via dialogue in home of interviewee, April 14th, 2015: Interviewees name withheld by mutual agreement

Interview by Author White by dialogue in church of present minister, October 23, 2016: Interviewees name withheld by mutual agreement.

Interview by Author White via e-mail, October 5th, 2017: Interviewees name withheld by mutual agreement

Interview by Author White via telephone conference, December 23rd, 2017: Interviewees name withheld by mutual agreement

Interview by Author White by dialogue in agreed meeting place, February 28th, 2018: Interviewees name withheld by mutual agreement.

Interview by Author White via e-mail, March 14th, 2018: Interviewees name withheld by mutual agreement.

Interview by Author White by dialogue, September 13th, 2018: Interviewees name withheld by mutual agreement.

OTHER BOOKS
WRITTEN BY DR. VELMA D. WHITE

Order your copy through: amazon.ca

1. *Redeeming Culture—The Other Side of the Coin* (Kindle ready)
Have questions regarding cultural practices and inclusion with Christian faith? This book addresses the distraction of syncretism that has crept into the church today. It challenges the reader to understand the confusion of syncretism (wordalivepress.ca).

2. *The Battle for Kingdom Identity—Our Spiritual Authority*
Seeing the struggle for identity from the beginning of human history, we are able to see how the battle has been settled for all who come to faith in Christ. This book focuses on our newfound identity in Christ. It helps the reader to gain an understanding with confidence about what it means to know your God-given identity as a believer (pagemaster.ca).

3. *Jesus Asked the Right Question*
A must read. Readers could not put it down. This book takes only thirty minutes to read. The reader becomes engaged in a dialogue while gaining insight and understanding of the redemption story of the Gospel in a nutshell. It is for the new believer. It is also for the seeker (pagemaster.ca).

CONTACT THE AUTHOR

E-mail: velforjesus@gmail.com

USA Address:

Att: Dr. Velma D. White
Velma White Ministries
4801 E. 41 Street, #106
Sioux Falls, SD 57110, USA

Canada Address:

Dr. Velma D. White
P.O. Box 793
Rocky Mt. House
AB, T4T 1A6, Canada

Donations for Velma White Ministries can be sent to the USA Address above.

CPSIA information can be obtained
at www.ICGtesting.com
Printed in the USA
BVHW040942301022
650516BV00002B/8

9 781098 039189